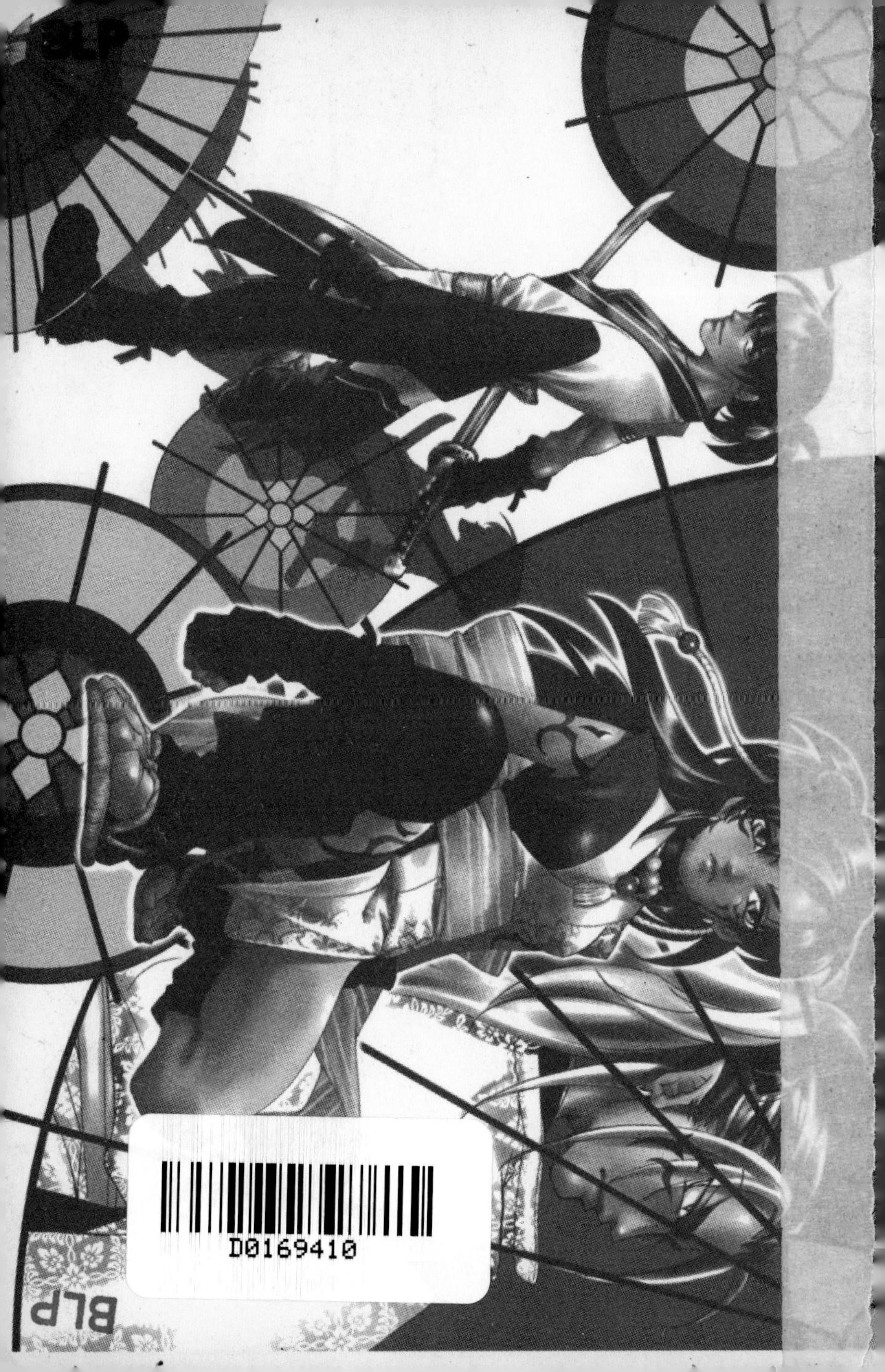

SW O RD
BY THE

sanami matoh presents

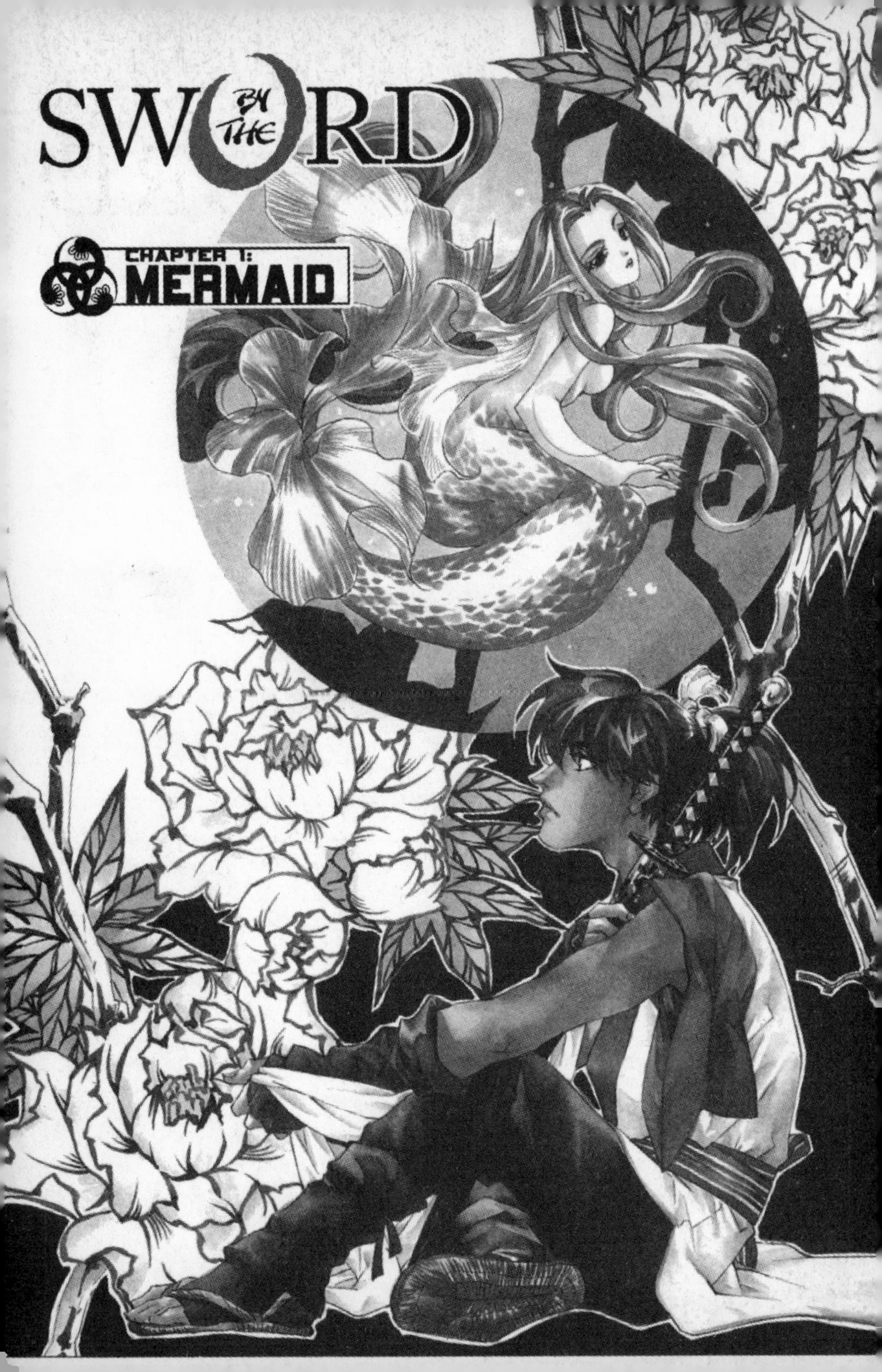
SWORD BY THE
CHAPTER 1:
MERMAID

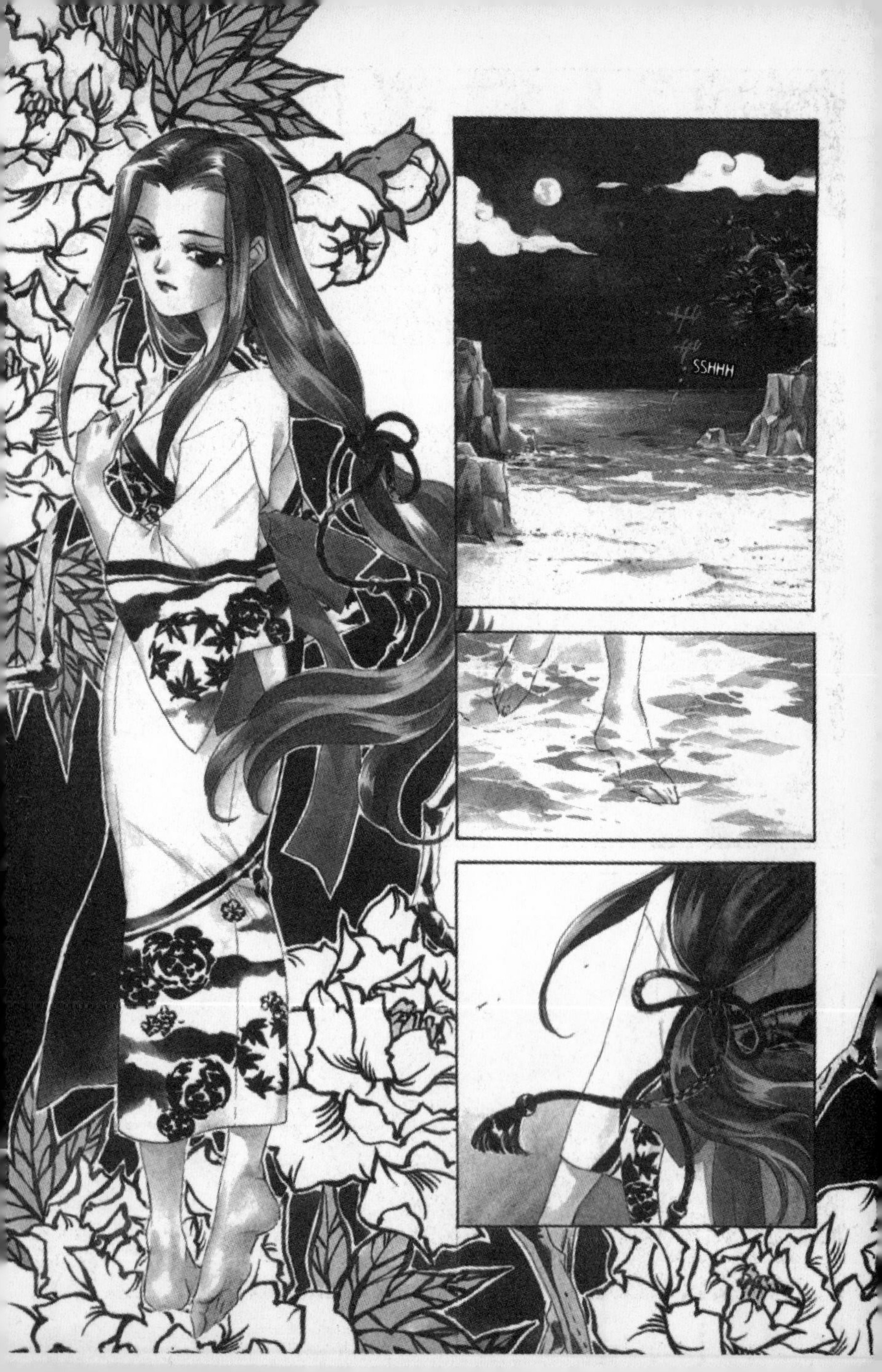
SSHHH

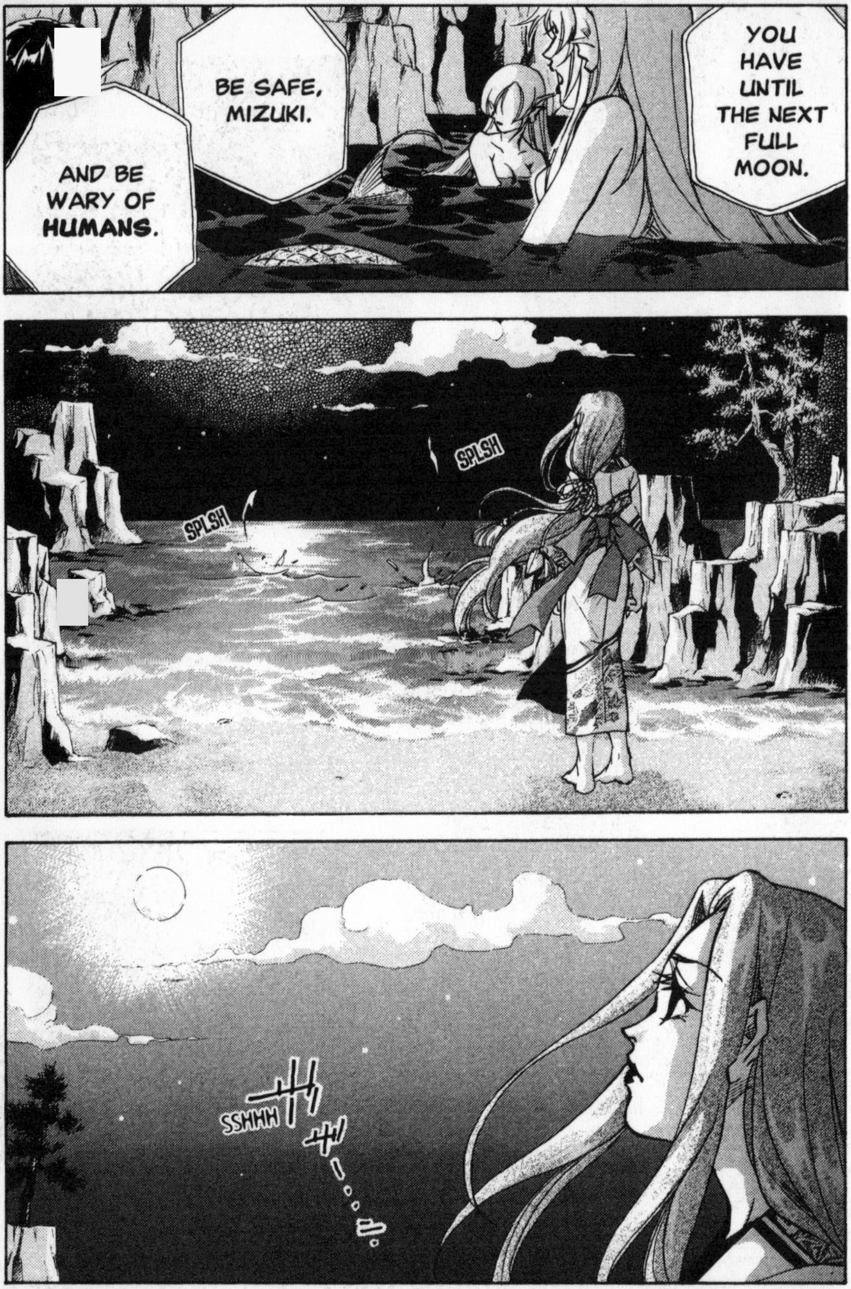
YOU HAVE UNTIL THE NEXT FULL MOON.
BE SAFE, MIZUKI.
AND BE WARY OF HUMANS.
SPLSH
SPLSH
SSHHH

COULDN'T TELL YA.

WELL, WHEN **IS** ONE GOING OUT?

WHAT?! NO SHIPS ARE GOING OUT TODAY?

LOOKS PRETTY CALM TO ME.

SSHHH

SEA'S BEEN ROUGH.

UH... WHY?

"ROUGH"?

DRAGON GOD, HUH?

THERE'S RUMORS GOING 'ROUND THAT THE DRAGON GOD IS UPSET.

FOR TEN DAYS NOW WE'VE BEEN TAKIN' SHIPS OUT ONLY TO HAVE 'EM TURN BACK AROUND. BEEN TERRIBLE FOR BUSINESS.

IT TURNS ROUGH ONCE YOU GET FARTHER OUT.

ASAGI!

THERE'S SOME DEAD GUY OVER THERE!

EVERYTHING ALRIGHT?

THUP

EVERYONE'S SAYING A DEMON DID IT.

THAT ARMBAND... YOU'RE A *KARININ*!

I GET IT.

SEE THIS? IF THIS WAS A DEMON, I NEED TO KNOW ABOUT IT.

HEY, WAIT YOUR TURN!

THERE'S RULES, Y'KNOW.

MIND IF I TAKE A LOOK?

'SCUSE US...

EVERYONE, CLEAR THE WAY! HE'S A *KARININ*!

IT LOOKS LIKE A DRIED-UP PIECE OF FISH OR SOMETHING!

He's all wrinkly.

YEESH

THIS IS A CORPSE?

THERE'S NO WAY A HUMAN DID THIS.

BRAVE GIRL, SHE'S NOT EVEN BATTING AN EYE... STILL, WHAT'S SHE LOOKING AT IT SO INTENTLY FOR?

FWP

UH-OH. GUESS I WAS STARING AT HER.

THAT THING LOOKED LIKE IT'D HAD THE ESSENCE SUCKED OUT OF IT. THERE'S NO WAY A HUMAN COULD'VE DONE THAT.

I'LL BET.

THERE WAS SOMETHING ABOUT THAT CORPSE. A KIND OF STRANGE AURA.

↰ HAD BEEN HIDING FROM THE CROWD

IT WAS ALMOST HUMAN... LOOK, I DON'T KNOW, ALRIGHT? IT WAS JUST STRANGE.

HMM.

STRANGE HOW?

10

RIGHT?

SO IT **WAS** KINDA DEMONIC, THEN?

YES, "KINDA." THAT'S WHAT MAKES IT STRANGE, YA MORON.

HM. THERE WAS A DEMONIC FEEL TO THAT AURA, BUT NOT ENOUGH FOR IT TO HAVE BEEN AN ACTUAL DEMON.

stare

...

KAEDE? WHAT'RE YOU LOOKING AT?

STILL, THERE WAS SOMETHING ALMOST FAMILIAR ABOUT IT...

OH COME ON.

ISN'T IT A LITTLE SOON FOR THAT?

WHAT?!

WHOEVER YOU ARE, GET OUT HERE **NOW** OR I'M GONNA FIREBALL YOUR ASS!

BWOOF

THERE'S SOMEBODY OUT THERE!

THP! D.P.

11

IT'S YOU. THE GIRL FROM EARLIER...

MY NAME IS **MIZUKI.**

YES. I HAVE A FAVOR TO ASK, KARININ.

I'M ASAGI. SO, YOU SAID YOU HAD SOMETHIN' YOU WANTED TO TALK ABOUT?

HUH?

A FAVOR?

WHAT?! YOU KNOW WHO DID THIS?

I WISH TO CATCH THE ONE RESPONSIBLE.

YEAH.

YOU SAW THE CORPSE, WHAT BECAME OF THAT MAN...

HE TOOK SOMETHING VERY IMPORTANT FROM US, AND WE MUST HAVE IT BACK. PLEASE, LEND US YOUR ASSISTANCE.

I DO.

UH-OH. IF THE SHIPS AREN'T LEAVING PORT, WE'RE GONNA HAVE TO STAY *HERE* FOR A WHILE. WHICH MEANS I'M GONNA HAVE TO EARN SOME MONEY TO BUY FOOD.

WELL, UH, HERE'S THE THING...

THOSE GUYS EAT A TON!

"THOSE GUYS"

HMMM

SCRTCH

13

IF THESE ARE NOT SUFFICIENT...

WOW. CORAL AND... PEARLS? IS THIS A REAL PEARL? I'VE NEVER SEEN ONE BEFORE.

I SHOULD TELL YOU, I CANNOT OFFER YOU MONEY.

I'D LIKE TO HELP YOU AND ALL, BUT...

cink

ONLY THESE.

WAAUGH!

SHP

I ALSO OFFER YOU MY **BODY**.

YOUR WHAT?

14

WHAT DO YOU THINK YOU'RE DOING?! YOU CAN'T JUST WALK AROUND SAYING THINGS LIKE THAT!

NO, NO! **NO!**

BMSH

BUT...

UH, YEAH. YOU TAKE CARE, NOW.

THANK YOU FOR ALL YOUR HELP.

VERY WELL. I WILL BE BACK IN THE MORNING.

WHAT IS WITH THIS GIRL?

BOW

I SEE.

THESE WILL BE MORE THAN ENOUGH! I'M SURE I'LL GET A LOT OF MONEY FOR 'EM.

WHAT DO YOU SAY WE PICK THIS UP TOMORROW, HUH?

L-LOOK, IT'S GETTING LATE.

BE SAFE, MIZUKI. AND BE WARY OF HUMANS.

DO NOT LET YOURSELF BE TAKEN IN BY MAN.

HE SEEMED DIFFERENT, THOUGH...

YOU ALRIGHT, ASAGI? YOU'RE BLUSHING.

HUH?!

=SIGH=

GOOD GOD. THE WOMAN THROWS HERSELF AT YOU AND YOU HAND HER HER **ROBE**? HOW STUPID CAN YOU GET?

URK

⬆ WAS OUTSIDE PEEKING IN

H-HEY! WHY DON'T YOU WATCH YOUR MOUTH, OLD MAN?!

AND SHE WAS SO PRETTY! I WOULD'VE BEEN ALL OVER THAT!

WHAT ABOUT **FUYO**, HUH?

WHAT HAS SHE GOT THAT I DON'T?!

stare

WH- WHAT'S WITH YOU?

(ASAGI SPEAKING)

HA HA

UH...AHEM! I JUST, I MEAN, YOU DON'T SEE SOMETHING LIKE, PEOPLE DON'T **SHOW** YOU SOMETHING LIKE THAT EVERY DAY! SO THAT WAS, UH...NICE?

GRRR

YEAH, I GUESS THAT'S PART OF IT.

You still got some growin' up to do.

HMM.

YOU'RE STILL JUST A KID.

IT AIN'T THE SAME, ASAGI. SURE YOU'VE GOT THE SAME **PARTS,** BUT A WOMAN LIKE THAT'S GOT SEX APPEAL.

GAH! DON'T TAKE YOUR CLOTHES OFF, IDIOT!

THAT'S IT!

HOW WOULD YOU KNOW?! YOU'VE NEVER EVEN SEEN WHAT I'VE GOT!

BWSH

I HAVE.

DON

17

EXCUSE ME.

THAT'S QUITE ALRIGHT. I'M FINE NOW THAT **YOU'RE** HERE.

IF YOU'RE NOT FEELING WELL, I HAVE SOME MEDICINE I COULD SHARE WITH YOU.

GRIN

GRAB

GRAARGH

THWMP

Hey, look!

I made me some **MAN** jerky!

HEH HEH.

HA HA HA HA HA!

WELL, WELL. CARRYING SOME PRETTY EXPENSIVE STUFF, ARE WE?

I TELL YA, IT'S JUST SO EASY BEIN' A THIEF! BWAHAHA!

THIS ORB HAS TURNED OUT TO BE PRETTY USEFUL.

IT'S WEIRD THAT A DEMON WOULD BE AFTER MONEY.

NOT UNHEARD OF, BUT WEIRD.

THE VICTIM WAS STRIPPED OF ANY VALUABLES, SAME AS YESTERDAY.

IT'S THE SAME M.O.

YOU'RE ASKING US FOR HELP, BUT IT'S CLEAR THAT YOU DON'T TRUST US.

I THINK IT'S ABOUT TIME YOU TOLD US WHAT YOU KNOW, MISSY.

OH.

C'MON, NOW. YOU MAKE IT SOUND LIKE **SHE'S** NOT HUMAN.

YOU WERE TOLD NOT TO TRUST HUMANS, IS THAT IT?

IT'S FAINT, BUT THERE'S AN AURA AROUND HER-- AND IT ISN'T HUMAN.

A MER-MAID...

IDIOT. SHE'S BEEN HIDING HER AURA THIS WHOLE TIME. TOOK YOU LONG ENOUGH TO NOTICE.

THE DRAGON KING? SO YOU'RE A **MERMAID**.

I'M THE DAUGHTER OF THE DRAGON KING.

DRAGON KING

WHY?

FOR MANY YEARS, MY FATHER HAS TAKEN HUMAN FORM AND VISITED THE TOWNS AND VILLAGES OF THIS LAND.

IT MEANS HE'S CURIOUS,

WHAT'S "IN QUISI-TIVENESS"?

BUT THE TRUTH IS, HE DOES IT OUT OF INQUISI-TIVENESS.

HE ALLEGES IT'S PART OF HIS DUTY AS LORD OF THE OCEAN...

HE USUALLY STAYS FOR THREE OR FOUR DAYS... BUT THIS TIME, HE WAS ATTACKED BY A BANDIT DURING HIS RETURN.

WELL, THAT'D EXPLAIN THE WEIRD AURA AROUND THAT CORPSE. IT WAS A MIXTURE OF ENERGIES, PART HUMAN AND PART THAT OLD COOT THE DRAGON KING.

THERE'S MORE. THE BANDIT STOLE SOMETHING FROM MY FATHER--THE DRAGON ORB.

"OLD COOT"? UH, YOU KNOW HIM?

I KNEW HIM, A LONG TIME AGO. SENILE OLD BASTARD'S EVEN OLDER THAN ME!

THE ORB IS AN OBJECT OF GREAT POWER. UNTIL NOW, MY FATHER HAS USED IT TO QUELL THE OCEANS, BUT...

SHOULD THE ORB BE HELD BY AN ORDINARY HUMAN...

AS AN OBJECT OF SUCH STRENGTH, A MEASURE OF POWER IS ALSO REQUIRED OF ITS POSSESSOR, THAT IT MAY BE WIELDED PROPERLY.

THE ORB REFLECTS THE WILL OF ITS POSSESSOR.

YES. SO LONG AS THE ORB REMAINS MISSING, THE OCEANS CANNOT BE CALMED.

SO THAT'S WHY THE SEA'S BEEN SO ROUGH LATELY? AND WHY THE BOATS CAN'T SAIL OUT TOO FAR?

WE CAN USE THIS.

WONDERFUL. IS THERE ANY WAY WE CAN LURE THIS GUY OUT INTO THE OPEN?

DEVOURING THE LIFE ESSENCE OF HUMAN AFTER HUMAN.

WELL, FOR STARTERS, IT'D POSSESS THE POOR SAP WHO WAS HOLDING IT. THEN IT'D PROBABLY GO ON A RAMPAGE,

THIS IS ALSO MY FATHER'S.

A **DEMON** ORB? WHOSE IS IT?

THE DRAGON ORB WILL RESPOND TO THE ENERGIES OF THIS ORB. I AM SURE IT WILL COME TO US.

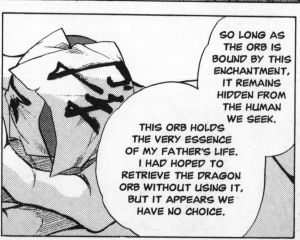

SO LONG AS THE ORB IS BOUND BY THIS ENCHANTMENT, IT REMAINS HIDDEN FROM THE HUMAN WE SEEK.

THIS ORB HOLDS THE VERY ESSENCE OF MY FATHER'S LIFE. I HAD HOPED TO RETRIEVE THE DRAGON ORB WITHOUT USING IT, BUT IT APPEARS WE HAVE NO CHOICE.

WHAT'S THE ENCHANTMENT FOR?

24

OK, HERE'S THE PLAN. WE LURE HIM OUT AFTER SUNDOWN...

WE ARE?

WE ARE ALMOST OUT OF TIME.

THAT WAY, NO ONE CAN SEE WHAT'S GOING ON.

ASAGI.

HEY, I DON'T BLAME YOU. A LOT OF PEOPLE DO TERRIBLE THINGS TO ANYONE WHO'S **NOT** HUMAN.

I APOLOGIZE FOR NOT TELLING YOU THE TRUTH.

HUH? OH, MIZUKI.

IF NEED BE, I COULD USE MY FATHER'S DEMON ORB WELL ENOUGH TO DEFEAT A HUMAN.

TO TELL THE TRUTH, THOUGH, I AM NOT WITHOUT POWERS MYSELF.

DO YOU REMEMBER OUR FIRST MEETING, WHEN I OFFERED YOU MY BODY AS PAYMENT?

NO. MY MERMAID SISTERS HAD TOLD ME THAT **THAT** WOULD BE THE MOST EFFECTIVE WAY OF SECURING HELP FROM A HUMAN MAN.

HEH.

SSHH

URK,

I REMEMBER. DON'T TELL ME YOU'RE STILL THINKIN' ABOUT...

YES. BUT IT DIDN'T.

SO, IF WORSE CAME TO WORST...

YOU SHOWED CONCERN FOR ME.

GENUINE CONCERN.

THE SUN'S ALREADY GONE DOWN.

WE SHOULD START GETTING READY.

OH, ASAGI...

IS IT POSSIBLE THAT YOU COULD EVER LIKE SOME- ONE LIKE ME?

UM, AHEM! UH...

. . . .

PWOOF

RIP

ACK! ぬ め っ loom

ALRIGHT, FESS UP. WHAT DO YOU THINK ABOUT HER?

← POSSESSED BY KURENAI

NAH. SHE FELL ASLEEP THE SECOND WE FINISHED EATING.

ZZZ

SO... SHE DIDN'T HEAR ANYTHING?

YOU'RE JUST LUCKY KAEDE WASN'T THERE.

SHE WOULD'VE GONE BALLISTIC.

VOICES CARRY, MORON. I DIDN'T HAVE TO EAVES-DROP.

H-HEY! WHAT'S THE BIG IDEA, EAVES-DROPPING LIKE THAT?!

OH...

≡PHEW≡

BUT WHAT?

I DON'T EVEN REALLY KNOW HER!

L-LOOK, YOU'VE GOT IT ALL WRONG!

TELL THE TRUTH, PIG! DO YOU LIKE MIZUKI OR NOT?!

I DON'T HATE HER, SO...YEAH, ALRIGHT, I GUESS I *DO* KINDA LIKE HER. BUT...

IF YOU MAKE KAEDE CRY, YOU'RE GONNA BURN!

WAUGH!

BWF!

AH! UH, NO, YOU SEE...

YOU SOUND PRETTY RELIEVED THERE, MISTER.

TWITCH

I...

SCUFF

HAND OVER THAT ORB.

HERE HE COMES!

scuff

THE ONLY ONE WHO'S GONNA BE HANDING OVER AN ORB...

BWSSH

TWITCH

BWFF

GRAAURGH!

IS YOU!

GAUGH!

B·SKSH

SKSSHH

ASAGI! NOW!

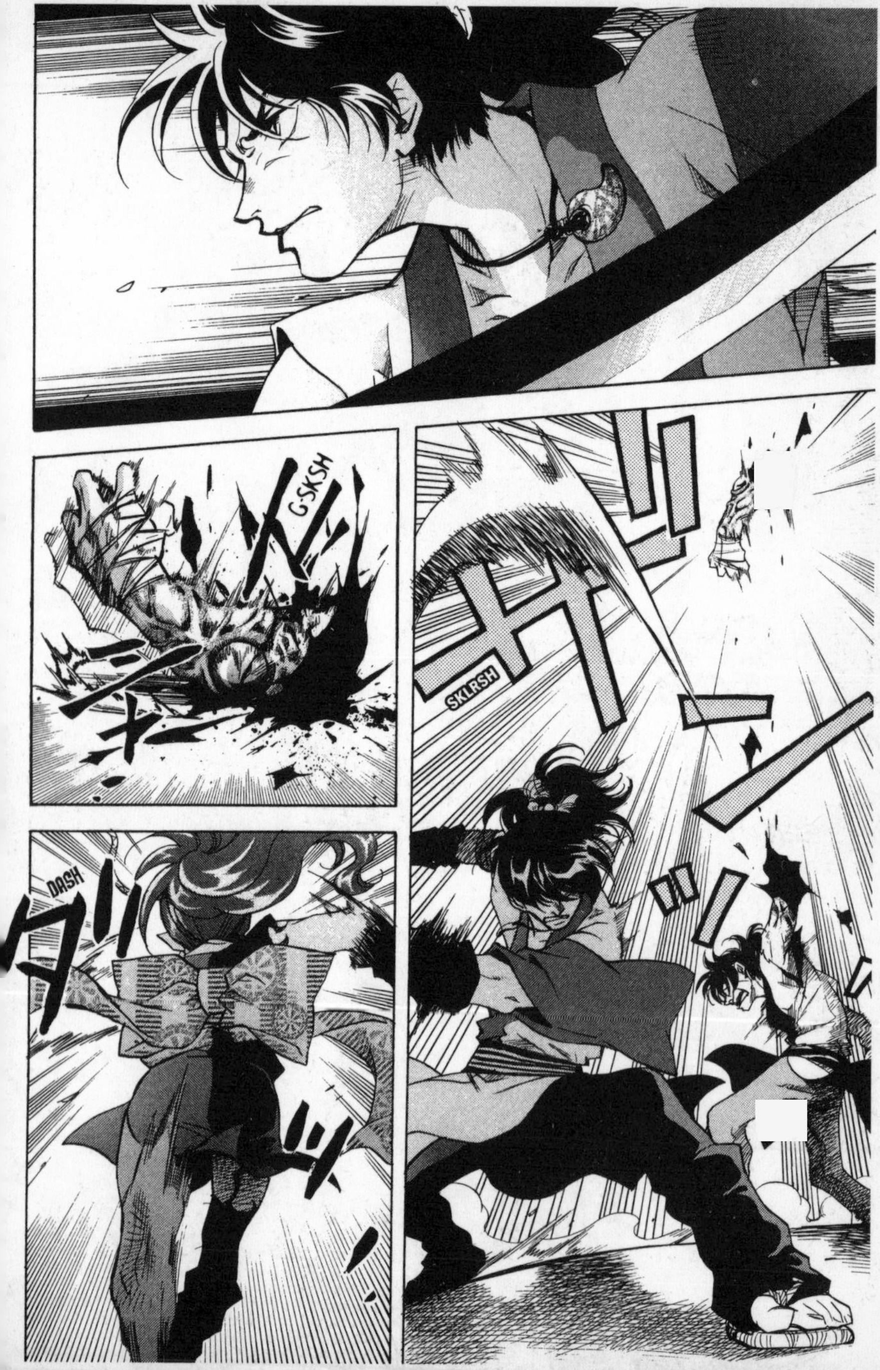

SKLRSH
G-SKSH
DASH

NO!
DON'T
TOUCH
THE
ORB!

KURENAI!

AAUGH!

GSKRKK

WHAT AM I SUPPOSED TO DO, THEN?!

WAIT! THE ORB STILL RETAINS THAT MAN'S EVIL!

IF YOU TOUCH IT, IT WILL POSSESS YOU, TOO!

KAEDE!

ASAGI...

SO IT SHOULD HAVE A WEAKNESS TO FIRE.

THE ORB HAS ITS ORIGINS IN WATER, RIGHT?

dash

KAEDE!

CRKK

AAURGH!

CRKK

CRKK

THE SWORD... IT'S EMITTING **FLAME!**

RRAAARGH!

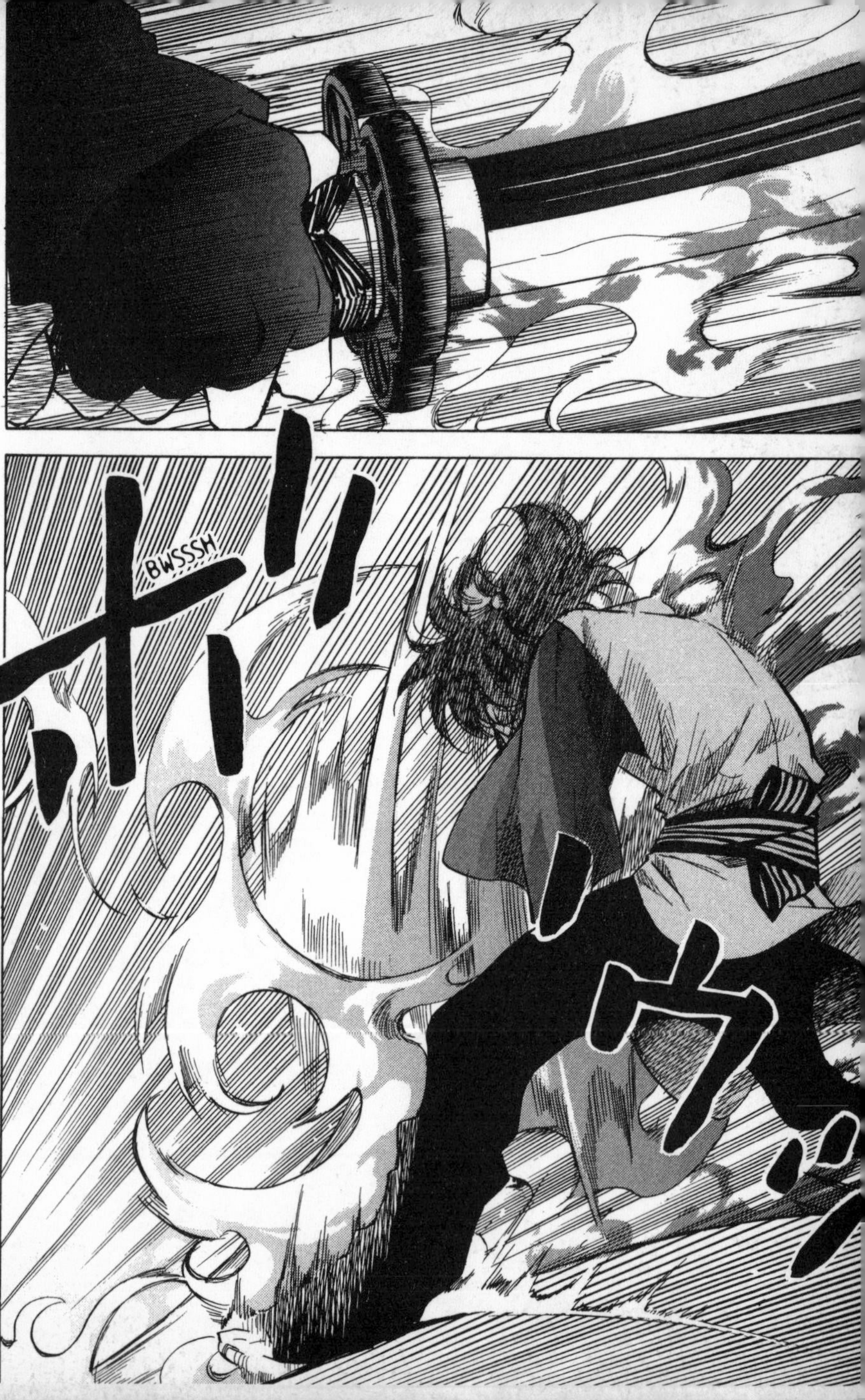
BWSSSH

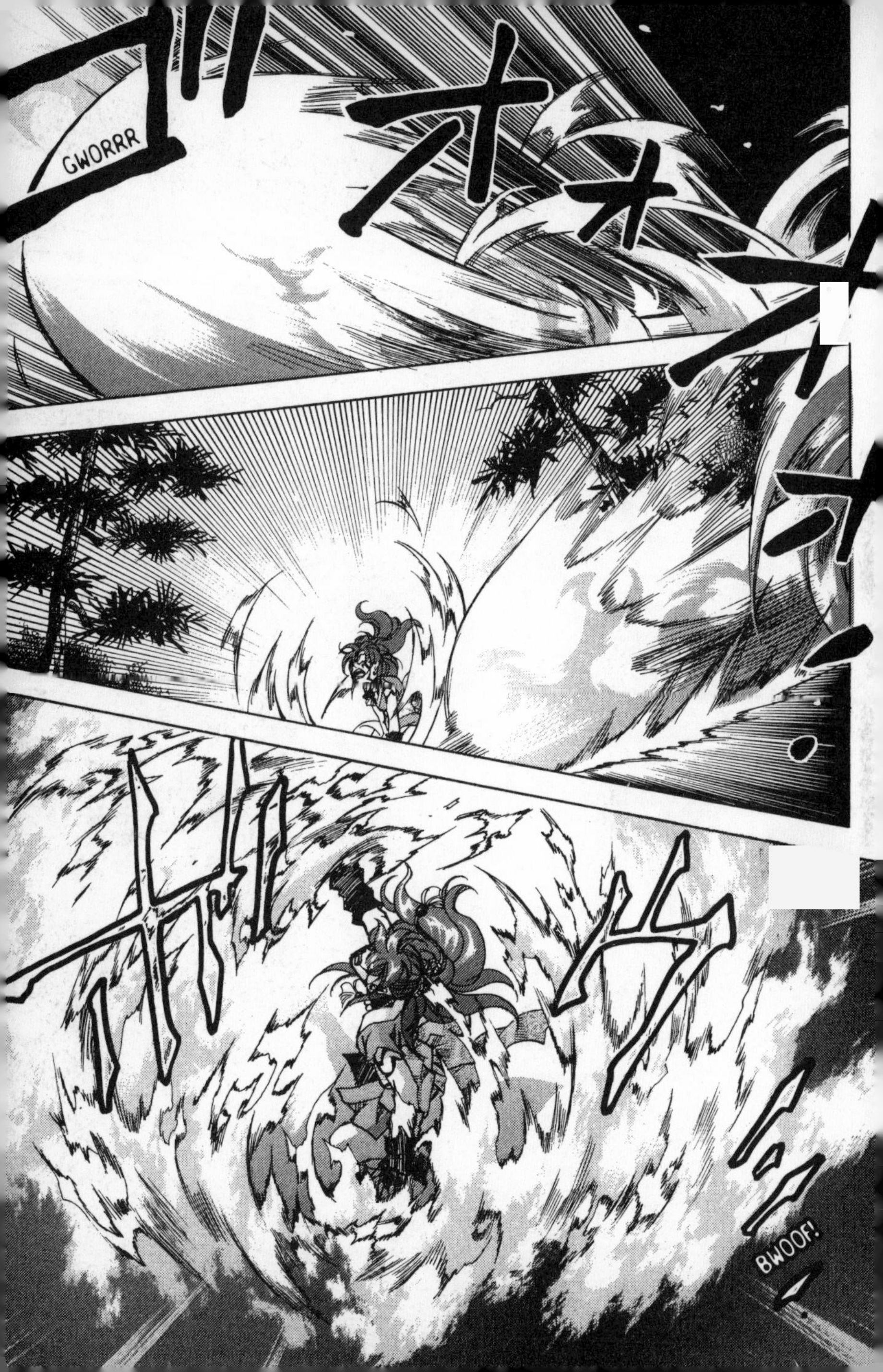
GWORRR
BWOOF!

ARE
YOU
ALRIGHT?!
SAY
SOMETHING!

KAEDE!

HNGH...

≡COUGH≡

≡COUGH≡

ASA... GI?

A LITTLE. I'M OK, THOUGH.

I'M SORRY I HAD TO DO THAT. DID IT HURT?

≡KOFF≡

≡PHEW≡

GEH♪

ASAGI! YOU BASTARD!

GLARE

WELL, SINCE YOU'RE THE DEMON OF FLAME, I FIGURED YOU COULD HANDLE IT.

Eheh.

THWACK

WHAT THE HELL IS WRONG WITH YOU? I COULD'VE BURNED TO DEATH!

AND WHAT IF I COULDN'T? YOU IDIOT!

HOW DID YOU EVEN DO THAT ANYWAY?

AND I FELT THE ENERGY IN MY BODY START TO BURN.

THEN, IT'S LIKE THAT ENERGY WENT INTO THE SWORD AND BECAME EVEN STRONGER.

I REMEMBER BEING ANGRY...

IT'S KINDA FUZZY.

40

THAT'S WHEN ALL THAT FIRE CAME OUT OF THE MOEGI.

IT WAS THE FIRST TIME THAT'D EVER HAPPENED.

AREN'T SO FAR-FETCHED AFTER ALL.

I GUESS THOSE RUMORS ABOUT GETTING "A HUNDRED AND ONE DEMONIC POWERS"

WELL, WELL.

IT WILL RETURN TO NORMAL ONCE IT RECEIVES MY FATHER'S ENERGY.

NOT TO WORRY.

OH, NO. IT'S **BLACK!** *That thing's been TOASTED.*

OH!

MIZUKI, IS THE ORB ALRIGHT?

I–I'M SORRY. I SHOULD'VE THOUGHT BEFORE I THREW ALL THAT FIRE AT IT...

I...

YOU WERE THINKING ABOUT KAEDE. YOU WANTED TO PROTECT HER, CORRECT?

I SAID I'D HELP HER LOOK FOR HER FATHER. AND IN MY MIND, I...

I MADE A PROMISE TO HER WHEN WE STARTED THIS JOURNEY.

I PROMISED THAT I'D STAY BY HER SIDE,

NO MATTER WHAT.

MY BODY RETURNS TO NORMAL ON THE NIGHT OF THE FULL MOON.

I HAVE TO GO BACK SOON.

OH, WELL. I SUPPOSE IT WASN'T MEANT TO BE.

≡SIGH≡

MY FATHER IS IN ONE OF THE CAVES TO THE SOUTH. PLEASE GO BY AND SEE HIM IF YOU HAVE THE CHANCE.

THANK YOU FOR RETRIEVING THE ORB.

HUH?

thp

THE FULL MOON? THAT'S TONIGHT.

44

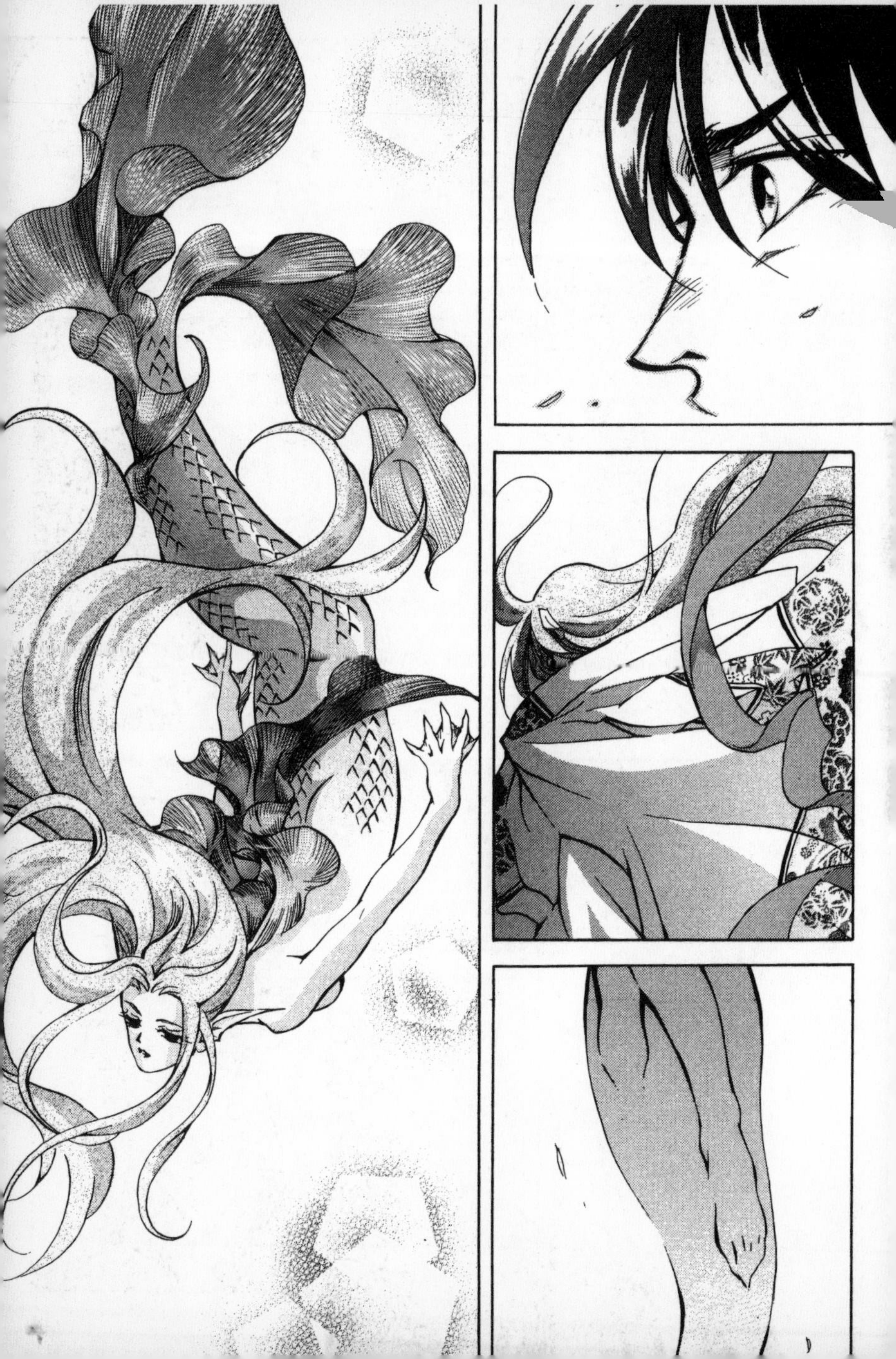

SPLSH

IT'S BEEN A WHILE, KURENAI. I'M SURPRISED YOU'RE STILL ALIVE.

YES, WELL, THIS OLD FOSSIL WOULD LIKE

TO THANK YOU FOR HELPING HIS DAUGHTER.

BACK AT YA, YOU OLD FOSSIL.

OH, I WAS HAPPY TO HELP-- SO THAT I'D HAVE YOU IN MY DEBT!

STUFF IT!

YOU TWO USED TO TALK ALL THE TIME, DIDN'T YOU?

FUYO? YES, INDEED. A SPLENDID WOMAN... FAR TOO GOOD TO BE YOUR WIFE!

BAP

WH-WHAT?! YOU MAKE DEMANDS FOR YOUR ASSISTANCE? YOU HAVEN'T CHANGED ONE BIT!

GRRR.

HEH.

TELL YOU WHAT. I'LL GIVE YOU A CHANCE TO RETURN THE FAVOR, HERE AND NOW. YOU REMEMBER FUYO?

YOU MUST KNOW A LOT ABOUT HER...

AND I WANT YOU TO TELL ME **EVERYTHING** YOU KNOW.

47

YOU ARE ALL FINISHED HERE, THEN?

KAEDE! WE'RE LEAVING.

DON'T YOU WANT TO SAY GOODBYE? HE'S RIGHT OVER THERE AT THE DOCK.

PLEASE GIVE ASAGI MY REGARDS. HAVE A SAFE JOURNEY.

NO, THAT'S ALRIGHT.

DO YOU LIKE ASAGI?

48

WHAT ABOUT YOU, KAEDE?

I'M **CRAZY** ABOUT HIM.

OF COURSE.

GOODBYE, KAEDE. TAKE CARE.

?

WHICH IS WHY FOR ME, IT WASN'T MEANT TO BE.

GRIN

SPLASH

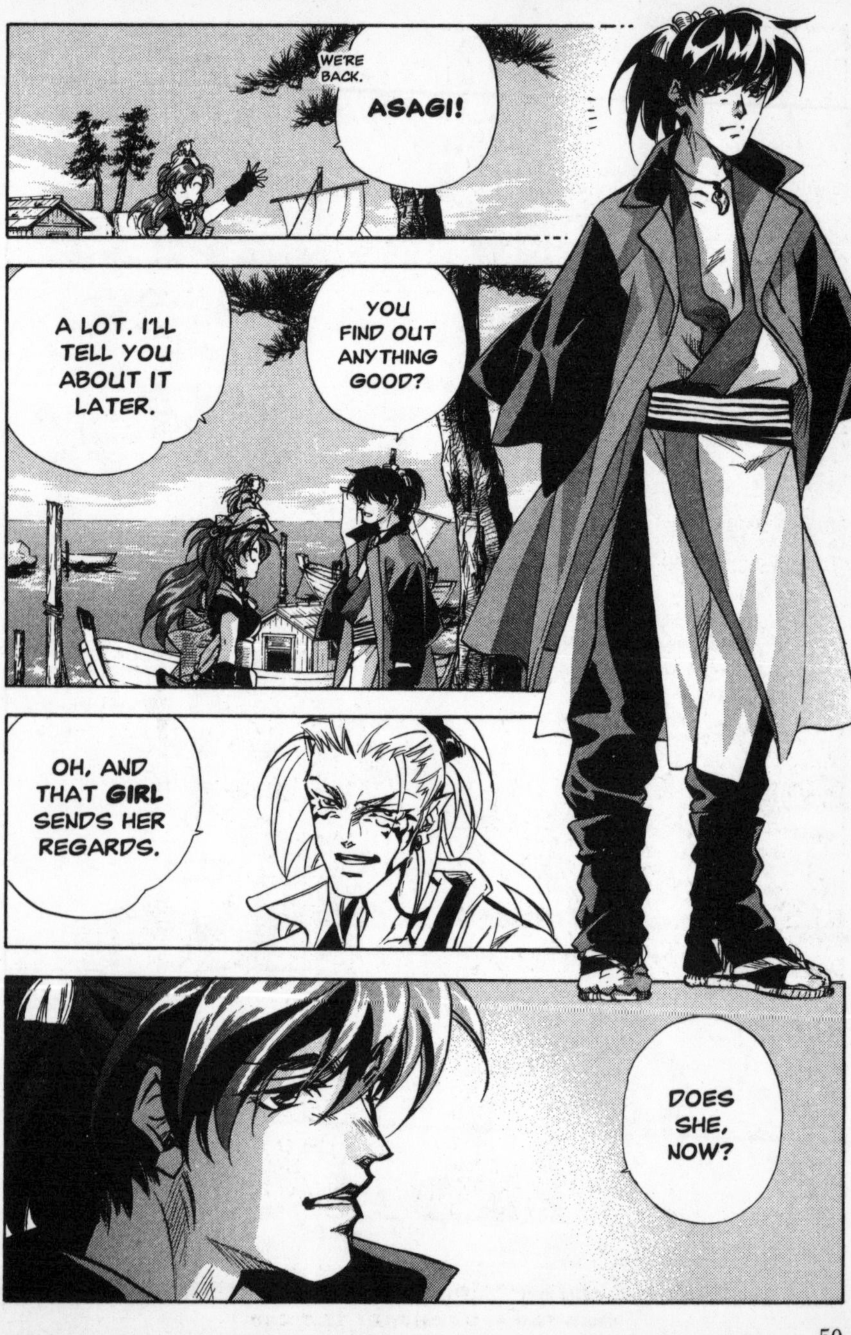
WE'RE BACK.
ASAGI!
YOU FIND OUT ANYTHING GOOD?
A LOT. I'LL TELL YOU ABOUT IT LATER.
OH, AND THAT GIRL SENDS HER REGARDS.
DOES SHE, NOW?

OK.

Alright.
LET'S MOVE IT, ASAGI. WE'RE HEADING TO THE MAINLAND.

THE MAIN LAND?

MAYBE I SHOULDA STAYED BEHIND.

YOU JUST ATE!

ASAGI, I'M HUNGRY.

CHAPTER 1: MERMAID / THE END

SWORD BY THE ORD

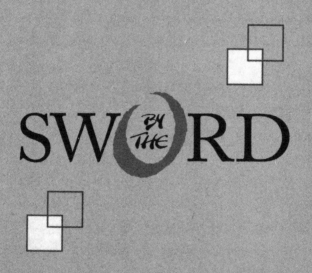

LORD GAZA.

A MESSENGER FROM LORD OZE HAS JUST DELIVERED THIS MISSIVE.

SO...

HE'S COMING AT LAST, EH?

YES, SIR.

FETCH **AOI** FOR ME, WOULD YOU?

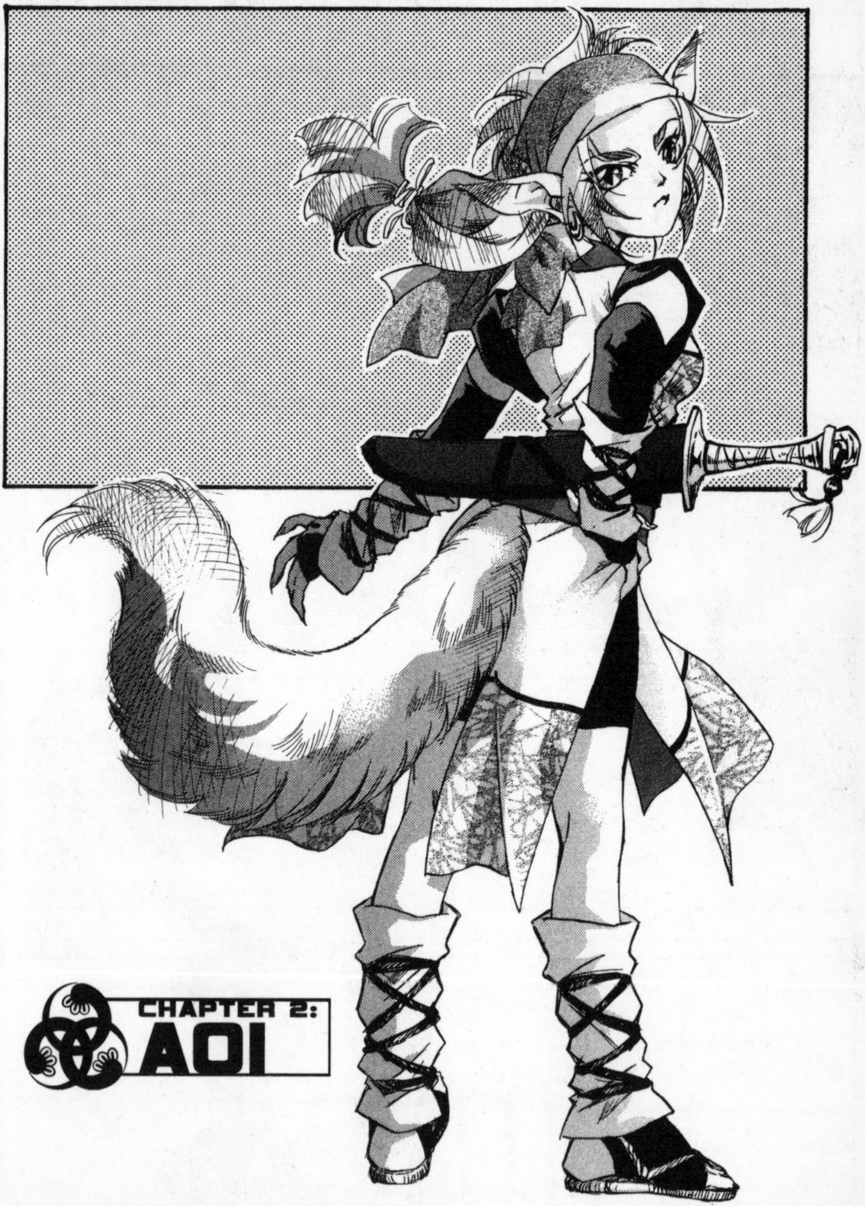

CHAPTER 2: AOI

AROUND HERE, AT LEAST.

YEAH, BUT IT'S PROBABLY THE ONLY KIND OF BOUNTY WE'RE GONNA GET.

HOW ABOUT THIS ONE? THE BOUNTY'S FIFTY SEN.

IT'S NOT ENOUGH. WE'D USE THAT UP IN THREE DAYS.

I WILL STRANGLE YOU.

RUSTLE

YOUR BOUNTY'S GONE UP.

HEY!

WHAT ABOUT THIS ONE? IT'S TEN **THOUSAND** SEN! WE'D BE SET!

ASAGI, I'M HUNGRY.

ALL WE HAVE TO DO IS MAKE IT THROUGH THE NEXT COUPLE OF DAYS AND WE'LL BE FINE.

SHUT UP!

WHY DO WE NEVER HAVE ENOUGH MONEY FOR FOOD?

I guess the answer's obvious, though...

≡SIGH≡

GROWWWWL

YOU SOUND MORE LIKE A CHILD THAN A MAN!

WILL YOU GIVE IT A REST ALREADY?! YOU'RE ALWAYS GOIN' ON ABOUT EVERY STUPID LITTLE THING!

I TOLD YOU NOT TO EAT SO MUCH ON THE SHIP, DIDN'T I? BUT NO!

OH YEAH? WHO DO YOU THINK **MAKES** ME HAVE TO GO ON ABOUT EVERY LITTLE THING, HUH?!

HEY, ASAGI! DAD!

SHUT UP!

UH-OH.

WAAUGH!

YIKES!

WI-WA-

THIS
COULD
BE
BAD.

OH,
NO.

IS SHE
A GIRL
OR A
BEAST?

TH-
THAT
WAS A
HOWL.

GRH...

RIIING

OW.

A-ALWAYS THIS HAPPENS! HE EATS SO MUCH. WHY HE CAN'T CARRY HIS OWN FOOD?!

FLAP

FLAP

FLAP

I DON'T EAT ONE **TENTH** THIS!

It's not fair.

EEK!

WHY IS IT SO DARK ALL OF A SUDDEN?

HM?

JEEZ. WHAT'S THE PROBLEM **THIS** TIME?

HUH?

THIS WAY.

WHAT WAS THAT?!

thp

KAEDE! IF YOU'RE THERE, ANSWER ME!

RUSTLE

HEY, IS SOMEONE THERE?

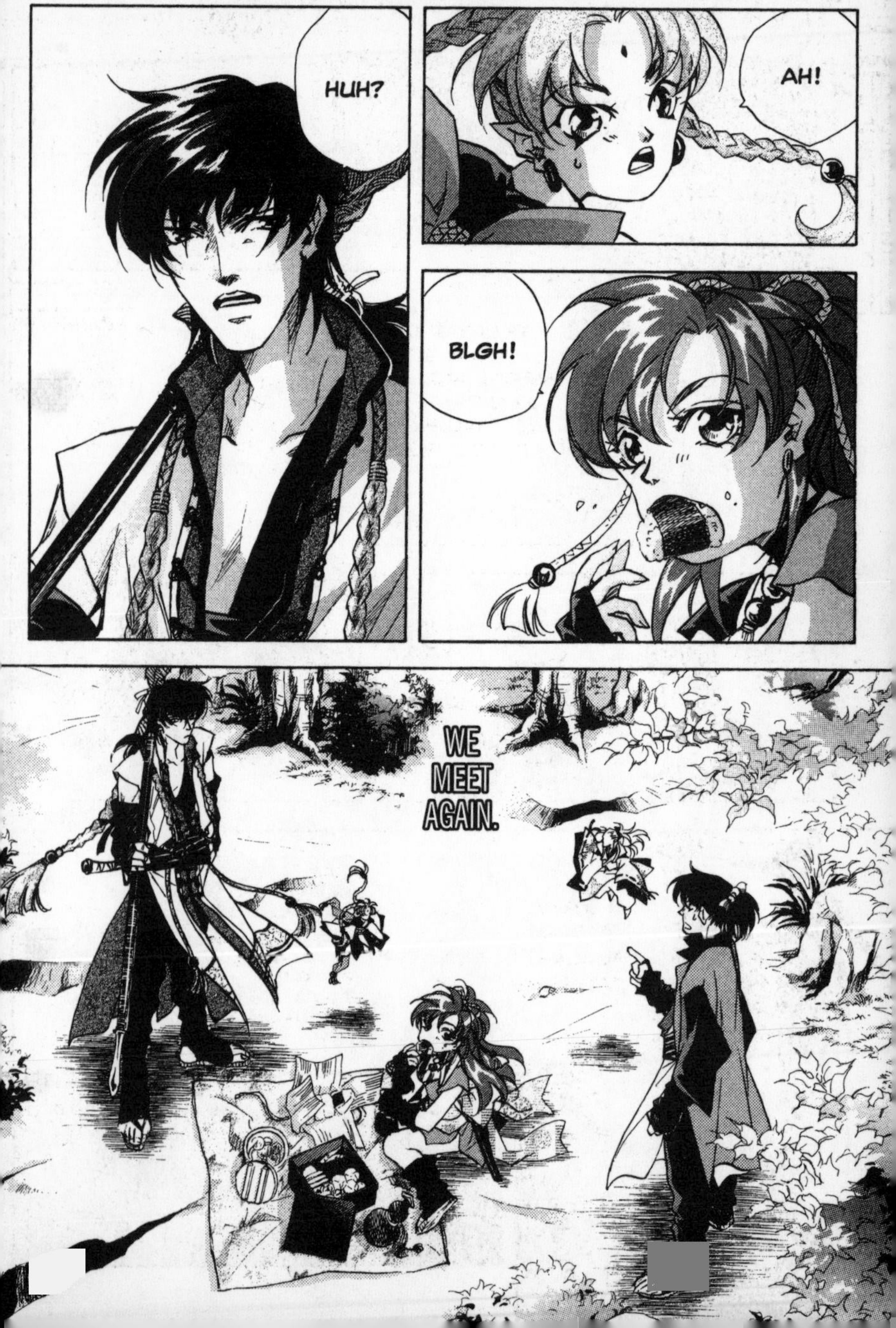
AH!
BLGH!
HUH?
WE MEET AGAIN.

THE DEMON-STONE?

WHOA. SOUNDS LIKE A PRETTY MANLY GUY.

DEMON WOLF

THE HEAD OF A CLAN OF **DEMON WOLVES** HEARD OF HIM AND CHALLENGED HIM TO A DUEL.

APPARENTLY, ONE OF MY ANCESTORS WAS KNOWN AS THE BEST SPEAR WIELDER IN ALL JAPAN.

THAT'S RIGHT.

MY ANCESTOR.

WISH I COULD'VE SEEN IT.

ANYWAY, WHO WON?

HE GAVE HIM THE DEMON-STONE.

AS A TOKEN OF FRIENDSHIP...

BUT THE WOLFMAN WAS IMPRESSED BY MY ANCESTOR'S SKILL AND STRENGTH OF CHARACTER.

THEY SAY THAT IF CARRIED BY A DEMON, IT'LL INCREASE HIS POWER SEVERAL **THOUSAND** TIMES.

SO WHAT KIND OF STONE IS IT?

THERE'S GOTTA BE SOMETHING SPECIAL ABOUT IT, RIGHT?

YUP. THE DEMONSTONE IS ALSO CALLED THE STONE OF TRANS- FERENCE.

SO IS IT JUST A NORMAL ROCK TO A HUMAN?

SHADDUP!

THIS WOULD BE THE "WISDOM OF THE AGED," RIGHT?

WELL, I'M GLAD TO SEE YOU HAVEN'T BEEN WASTING YOUR TIME ALL THESE YEARS.

YOU'RE TELLING ME. I'VE BEEN GETTING RID OF DEMON ORBS BY SLAPPING CHARMS ON THEM, OR PUTTING THEM IN URNS AND TAKING THEM TO PRIESTS TO TAKE CARE OF.

THAT COSTS MONEY.

HUH. I GUESS THAT'S WHY IT'S CALLED THE STONE OF **TRANS-FERENCE.** SURE WOULD COME IN HANDY...

NO. IF THE STONE IS ATTACHED TO A WEAPON, IT WILL TRANSFER ITS DEMONIC ENERGY TO THE WEAPON ITSELF, MAKING IT POWERFUL ENOUGH TO DESTROY A DEMON ORB!

WELL, THAT'S THE THING...

HUH. BUT WAIT. IF ONE OF YOUR ANCESTORS ORIGINALLY GOT THE STONE, THEN SHOULDN'T **YOU** HAVE IT?

THERE AREN'T MANY THAT CAN, THOUGH.

DEPENDS ON THE PRIEST.

WHOA, **PRIESTS** CAN GET RID OF DEMON ORBS?

FLASHBACK

I HAVE SOMETHING **IMPORTANT** TO TELL YOU.

ONCE YOU'VE FINISHED YOUR TRAINING AND BECOME A *KARININ*, THE FIRST THING YOU MUST DO IS COME STRAIGHT HOME.

NOW THEN, SUOH.

SUOH AT AGE TEN

OK, GRANDPA. I'LL COME RIGHT BACK!

I FINALLY RETURNED HOME THE OTHER DAY...AND MY GRANDFATHER PRETTY MUCH EXPLODED.

BWAHAHA! LOOK OUT CHINA, HERE I COME!

HEY, WATCH OUT!

AND ENDED UP GOING TO **CHINA** FOR MORE TRAINING.

UNFORTU- NATELY, I FORGOT ALL ABOUT IT...

WHAT WAS **THAT** FOR, YOU CRAZY OLD MAN?!

WAUGH!

KA-POW!

OOPS

NOW THAT YOU MENTION IT...

GRR

WHAT DID I TELL YOU? I SAID TO COME STRAIGHT HOME!

IMBECILE! NOW YOU DECIDE TO COME BACK?!

I WAS FINALLY TOLD THAT THE STONE WAS IN THE WOLF VILLAGE ON THIS MOUNTAIN.

SO ANYWAY, AFTER BEING LECTURED (AND BEATEN REPEATEDLY),

TALK ABOUT LUCK.

THERE'S A WOLF CLAN HERE?

COME AGAIN?!

SQUEEZE

AAAA!

I'M SORRY!

I WAS ALSO TOLD TO GO GET IT, WHICH IS WHY WE'RE HERE. BUT...

BUT WE GET LOST! **REALLY** STUPID!

WHAT? LOOK, I DON'T WANT ANY TROUBLE...

TELL YOU WHAT, SUOH. WE'LL HELP YOU FIND THE VILLAGE IF YOU'LL LET ME TALK TO THEIR LEADER.

YOU'RE NOT JUST TAKING ADVANTAGE, RIGHT?

DO YOU GUYS ALWAYS EAT THIS MUCH?

I'M STILL EATING.

THIS IS **LESS** THAN USUAL.

TREATING

WELL, I GUESS THAT'S ALRIGHT, THEN. BY THE WAY...

RELAX. I JUST WANT TO ASK HIM SOMETHING.

DID YOU HEAR? A **HUMAN** IS COMING TO THE VILLAGE.

GENJI!

HE'S COMING FOR THE STONE!

HMPH.

SO IT'S FINALLY HAPPENING.

IT'S FOOLISH TO HAND IT OVER TO SOME HUMAN!

IT BELONGS TO US. IT SHOULD BE USED BY US!

WELL, I MEAN...

THE STONE IS A TREASURE. WHY SHOULD WE JUST LET IT GO? AARGH, WHAT IS OUR LEADER THINKING?!

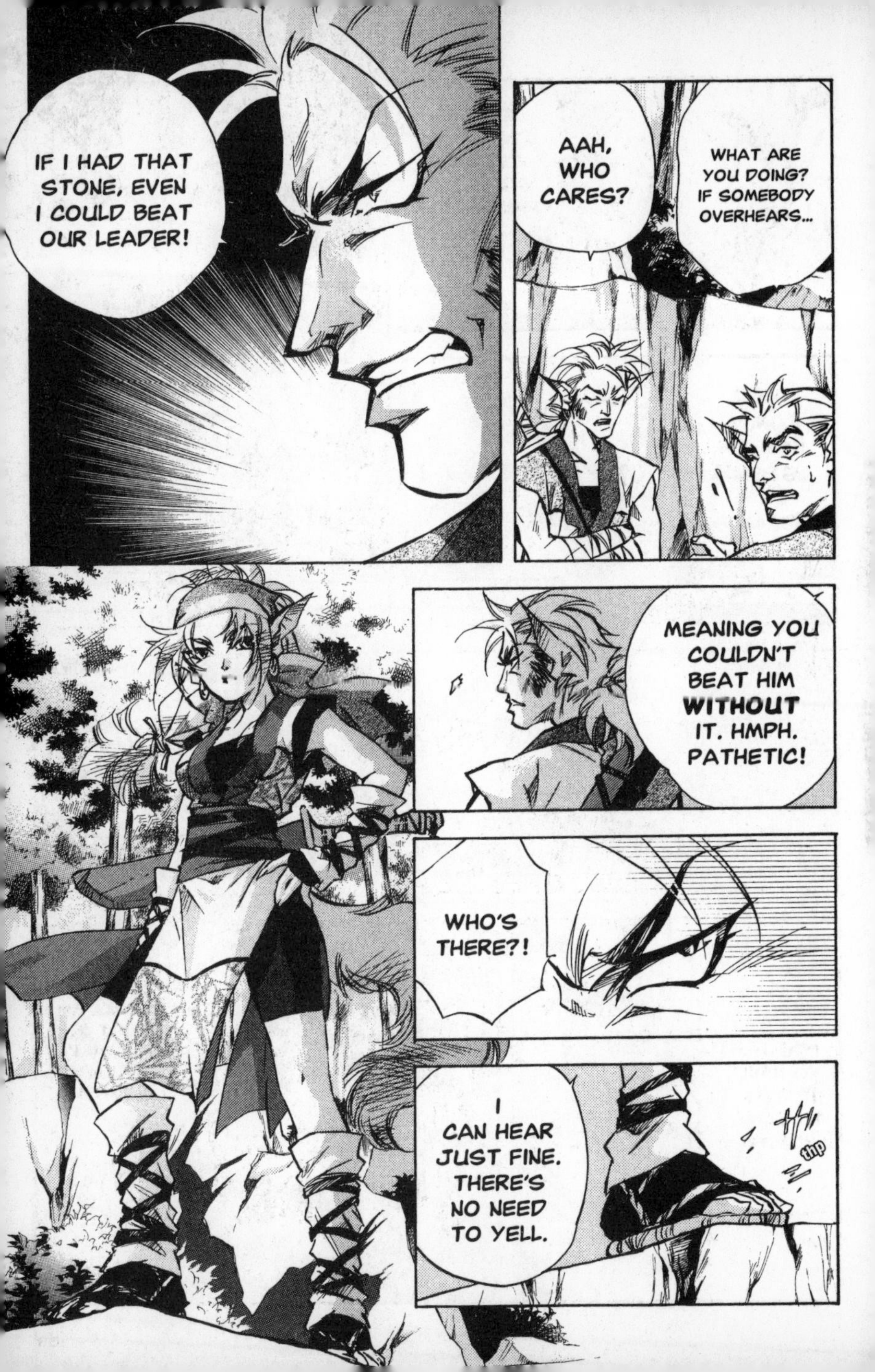
IF I HAD THAT STONE, EVEN I COULD BEAT OUR LEADER!
AAH, WHO CARES?
WHAT ARE YOU DOING? IF SOMEBODY OVERHEARS...
MEANING YOU COULDN'T BEAT HIM WITHOUT IT. HMPH. PATHETIC!
WHO'S THERE?!
I CAN HEAR JUST FINE. THERE'S NO NEED TO YELL.
thp

DON'T GO STIRRING UP TROUBLE WITH SOME HALF-BAKED IDEA.

THE FATE OF THE STONE HAS ALWAYS BEEN DECIDED BY THE **CLAN**, GENJI.

NOT LONG.

MA'AM! HOW LONG HAVE YOU BEEN THERE?

HMPH. THAT'S SOME MOUTH YOU'VE GOT ON YOU, YOUNG LADY.

I DON'T CARE IF YOU **ARE** OUR LEADER'S DAUGHTER-- THAT DOESN'T MEAN YOU GET TO ORDER ME AROUND.

GRAB

GET YOUR FILTHY HANDS OFF ME!

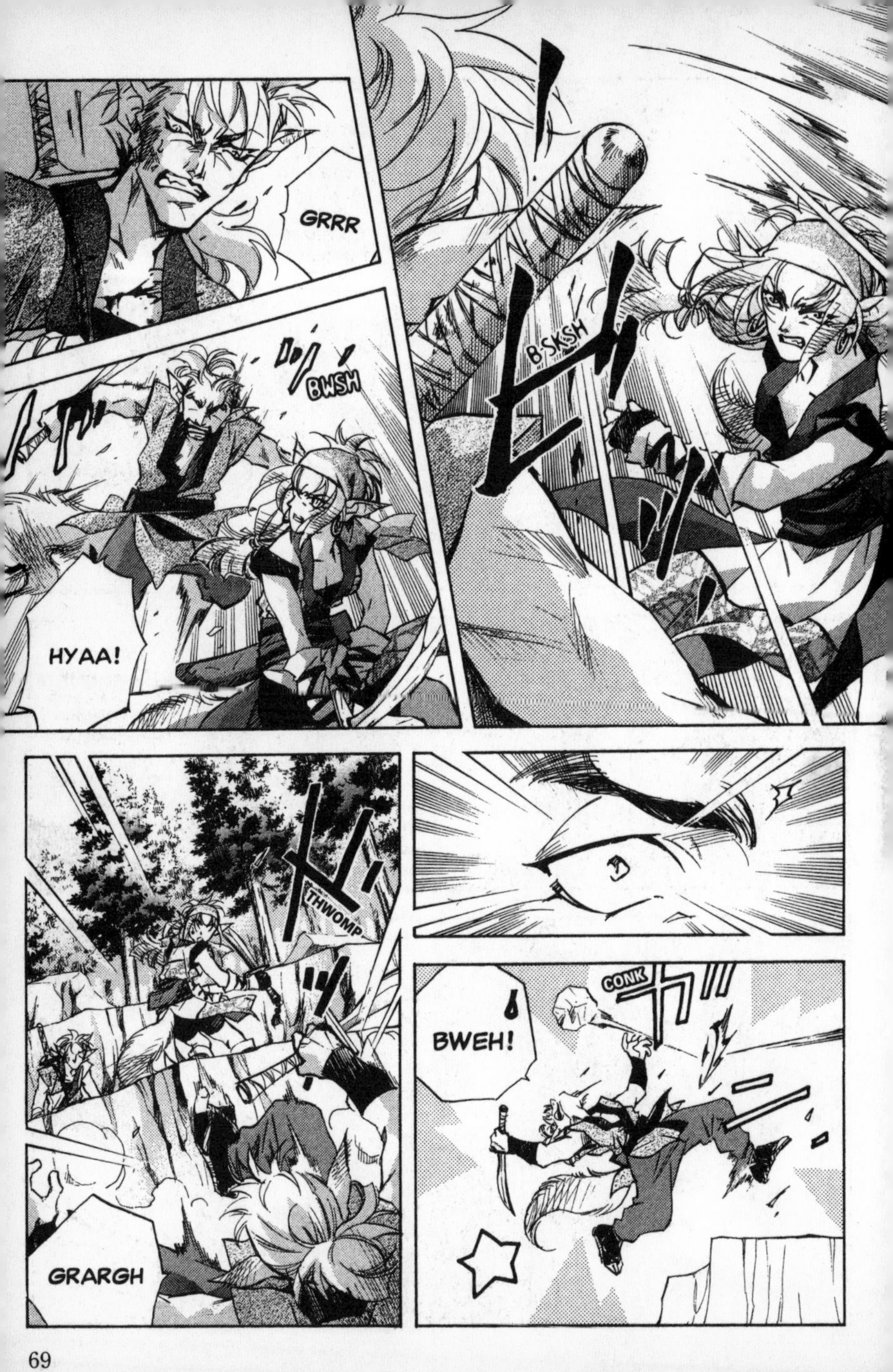
BSKSH
GRRR
BWSH
HYAA!
CONK
BWEH!
THWOMP
GRARGH

TWO GUYS AGAINST ONE GIRL? THAT'S NOT NICE.

WHO THE HELL ARE YOU?!

BULLS-EYE.

PAT

PAT

PISSING ME OFF!

BNSH

YOU'RE STARTING TO PISS ME OFF, HUMAN.

IS THAT SO?

GRAB

UH-HUH. YOU'RE REALLY...

CRACK!

HUH?

GRAAUGH!

SKSSSHHH

C-COME ON, GENJI! LET'S GET OUT OF HERE.

I'LL TELL YOU WHAT'S PISSING ME OFF-- THAT DUNG HEAP YOU CALL A FACE.

HUH? YES, I'M FINE.

ARE YOU ALRIGHT?

GRR

thp

GRIN

YOU SHOULDN'T HANG AROUND GUYS LIKE THAT, YOU KNOW.

I DON'T UNDER-STAND...

Y-YES.

OH. YEAH.

PRETTY SHARP.

THERE. THAT ARMBAND MEANS YOU'RE A *KARININ*, RIGHT?

IF YOU'RE GONNA PICK A FIGHT, AT LEAST MAKE SURE YOU CAN HANDLE YOURSELF.

YOU OUGHTA THINK TWICE BEFORE SAYIN' SOMETHING YOU'LL REGRET.

YOU KNOW,

ARE YOU SU--

WHAT?!

SUOH HERE JUST DOESN'T HAVE MUCH TACT.

CALM DOWN. HE DIDN'T MEAN ANYTHING BY IT.

HEY! ARE YOU TRYING TO PICK A FIGHT WITH ME?!

EASY NOW.

HUH? NO, MY NAME'S ASAGI.

Sorry.

YOU MEAN YOU'RE NOT SUOH?

GEH!

THEN THAT MEANS...

≡SIGH≡ NOW WHAT?

SUOH! THANK GOODNESS YOU'VE FINALLY COME.

HOW I'VE WAITED FOR THIS DAY!

THAT PREVENTED ME FROM GETTING HERE SOONER.

YEAH, SORRY ABOUT THAT. THERE WERE SOME, UH, UNEXPECTED **DIFFICULTIES**

SOME WHAT?

I THOUGHT YOU JUST FORGOT!

IF YOU'LL EXCUSE ME.

THIS IS MY DAUGHTER, AOI.

AH, THANK YOU.

FATHER, I'VE BROUGHT THE STONE.

THIS IS THE DEMON-STONE.

HUH?

HEY!

FWP

HMPH

BUT NOW WE CAN FINALLY BRING IT OUT INTO THE OPEN.

WE USUALLY KEEP IT SAFELY HIDDEN AWAY,

HUH. IT LOOKS A LITTLE BROWN, TOO.

WOW. WHAT A BEAUTIFUL PALE BLUE...

UH, "MATCH"?

I HAVE HEARD FROM YOUR GRANDFATHER, LORD OZE, THAT YOUR SKILL WITH THE SPEAR IS UNPARALLELED. I AM LOOKING FORWARD TO THE MATCH.

HUH?!

YES. YOUR MATCH AGAINST ME.

YOU? AND ME?

SURELY YOUR GRAND-FATHER HAS INFORMED YOU OF THIS!

WIN, AND THE STONE WILL BE YOURS. LOSE, AND IT SHALL NOT.

I'M GONNA KILL THAT OLD MAN!

UH... YEAH.

HEY, IT LOOKS LIKE THE MATCH IS GONNA BE TOMORROW AFTERNOON!

ALRIGHT! I'M DEFINITELY GOING!

IT'S BEEN A LONG TIME SINCE WE'VE SEEN THE CHIEF PULL OUT HIS SWORD, HUH?

YEAH... HEY, YOU KNOW SOMETHING?

ARE YOU GOING, GENJI?

THERE'S NO WAY HE CAN BEAT THE CHIEF, THOUGH.

YEAH. AND I HEARD HE'S REALLY GOOD.

THE GUY HE'S FIGHTING IS YOUNG, RIGHT?

THE DEMONSTONE IS USUALLY HIDDEN AWAY SOMEWHERE... BUT FOR THE MATCH TOMORROW THEY'RE PUTTING IT ON THE ALTAR, RIGHT OUT IN THE OPEN.

THIS IS GONNA BE GREAT!

AND RIGHT IN OUR REACH...

chatter

chatter

chatter

IT'S A CHANCE TO SEE MY FATHER IN BATTLE AGAIN.

THEY'VE ALL BEEN LOOKING FORWARD TO THIS.

WOW. A LOT OF PEOPLE SHOWED UP, HUH?

THEY SAY THAT WHEN IT COMES TO THE SWORD, NO ONE CAN EVEN COME CLOSE!

EVEN I'VE HEARD THE RUMORS ABOUT HIM.

(KURENAI SPEAKING)

YES. VERY.

YOUR DAD'S PRETTY GOOD, THEN?

IT'S NOT YOUR LUCKY DAY, SUOH.

HA! THAT'S GREAT!

IZUMO?

RIGHT NOW, WE'RE HEADED FOR IZUMO.

WE'RE PRAC-TICALLY THE SAME AGE.

JUST CALL ME ASAGI, HUH?

UM, MISTER ASAGI?

OK... WHERE ARE YOU ALL TRAVELING TO, ASAGI?

OF COURSE WE HAVE.

THAT'S WHY WE CAME HERE. WE WERE HOPING SOMEONE MIGHT HAVE HEARD OF HIM...

THE THING IS, WE DON'T KNOW WHERE HE IS.

THAT'S RIGHT. WE'RE LOOKING FOR **SEIGA**, A FAMOUS MEMBER OF A WOLF CLAN LIKE THIS ONE.

HE'S MY FATHER'S YOUNGER BROTHER-- MY UNCLE.

UH... YEAH.

REALLY?!

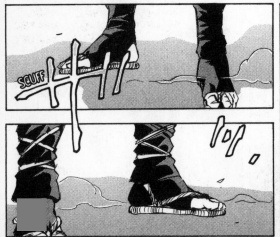

SCUFF

THE MATCH IS ABOUT TO START.

WHAT DO YOU SAY WE PICK THIS UP LATER?

BE GENTLE, HUH?

THE STONE IS THERE, ON THE ALTAR.

HEH, YEAH, RIGHT.

OH, I PLAN ON IT.

BEAT ME, AND IT'S YOURS TO TAKE.

VERY WELL.

THMP

LET US BEGIN!

krkk

kaSHING

GRGH

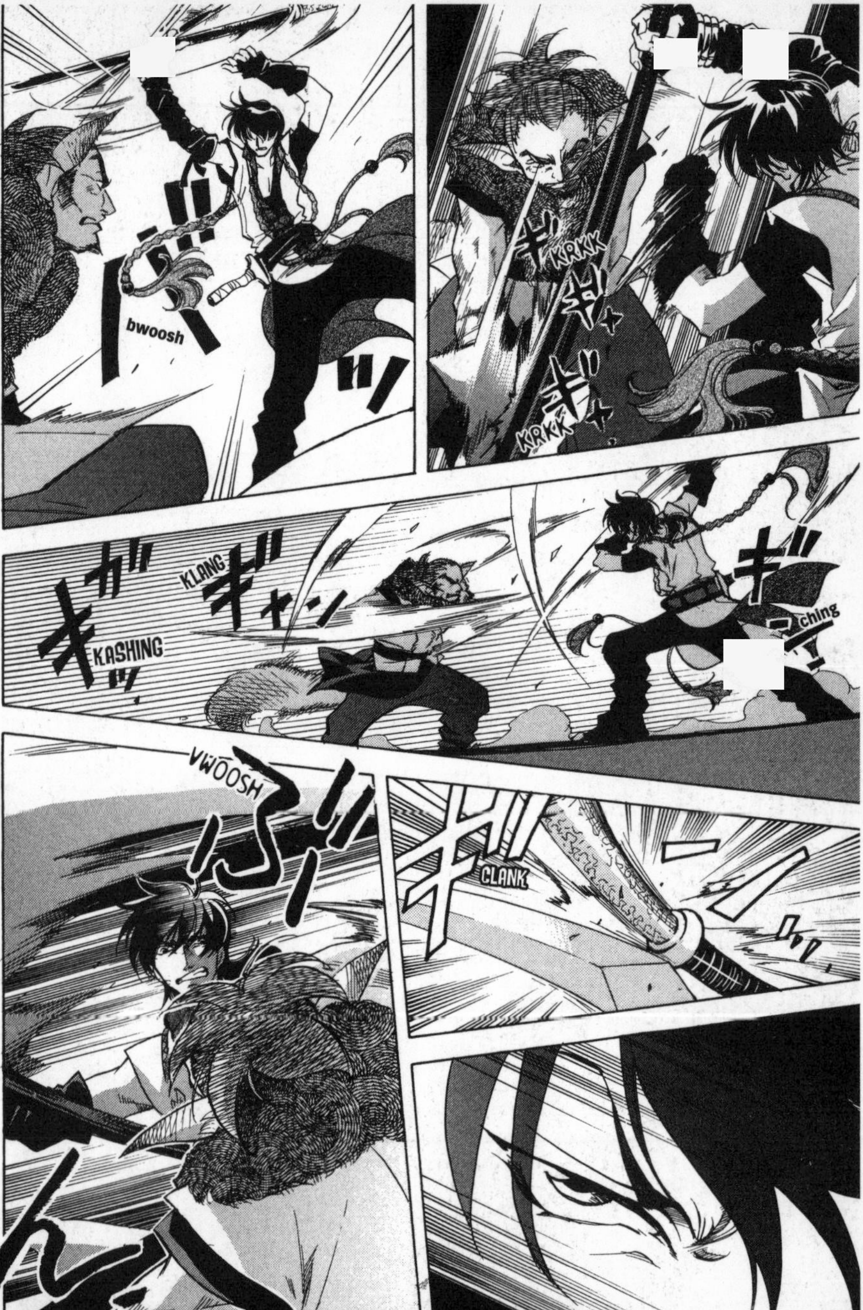
KRKK
KRKK
bwoosh
ching
KLANG
KASHING
CLANK
VWOOSH

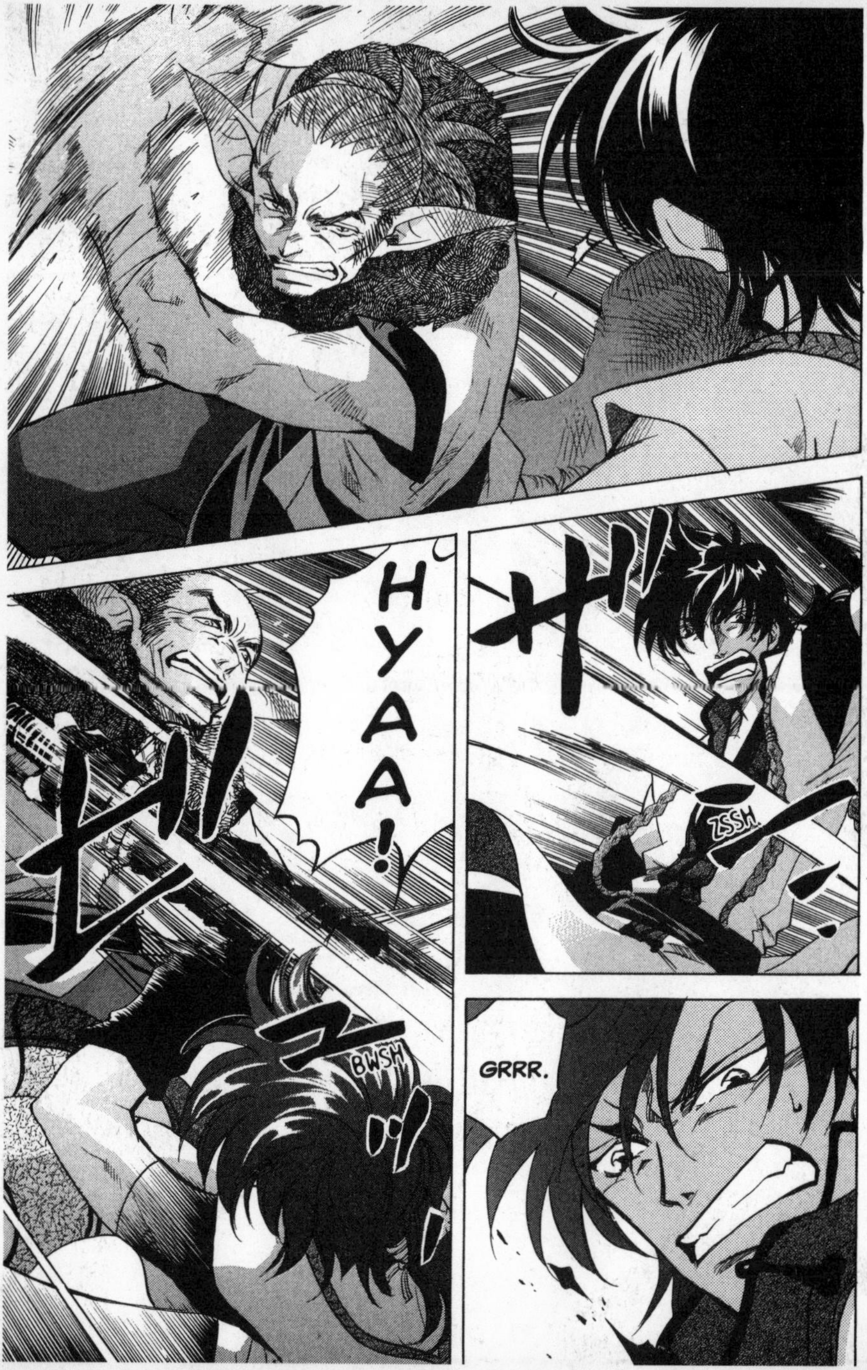
HYAA!
ZSSH
BWSH
GRRR.

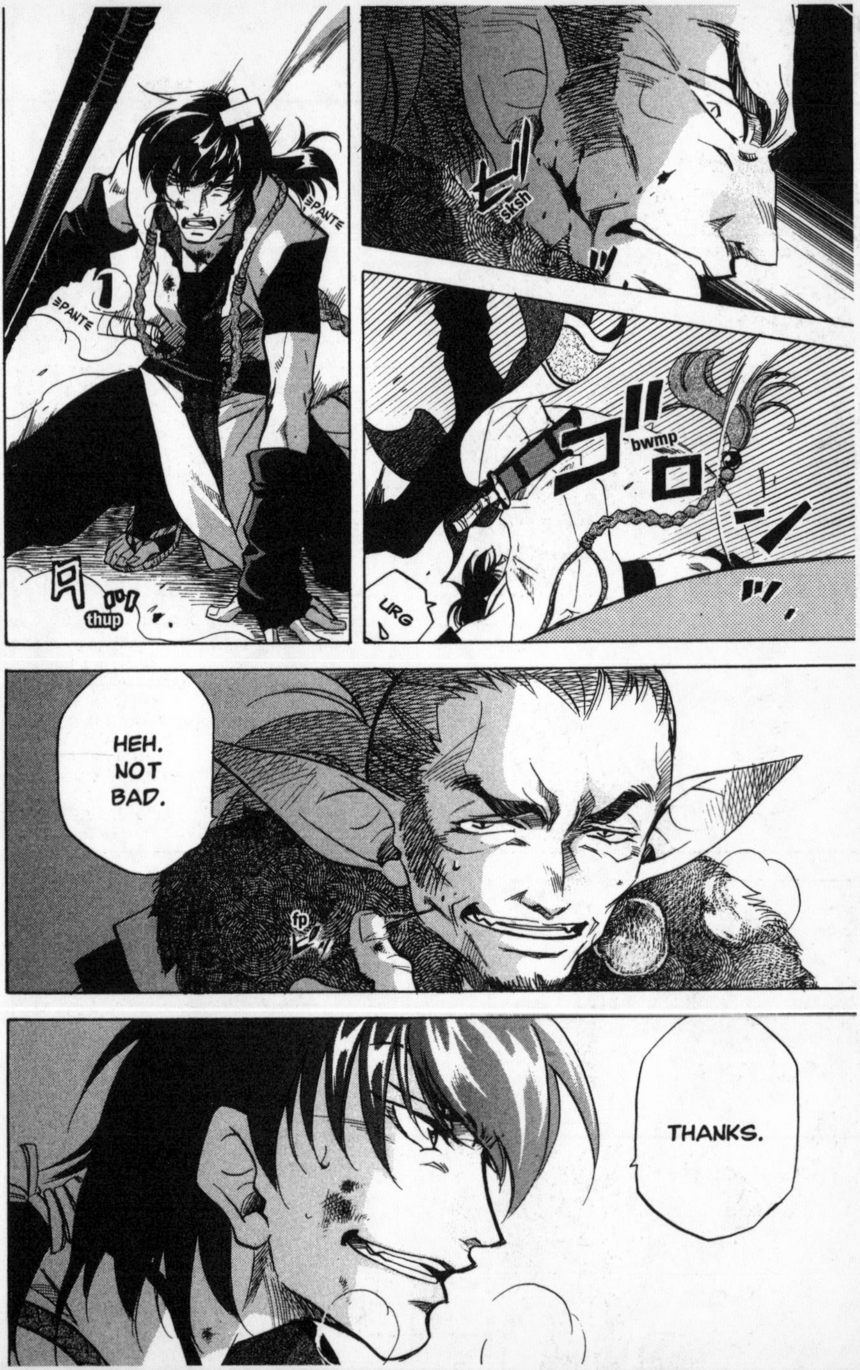
sksh
bwmp
URG
PANTE
PANTE
thup
HEH. NOT BAD.
fp
THANKS.

IS SUOH GONNA BE ABLE TO PULL IT OFF?

MAN, THAT WOLF GUY'S REALLY GOOD.

WHAT IS IT, AOI?

THERE'S SOMEBODY STANDING BEHIND MY FATHER... WHO IS THAT? DOESN'T HE KNOW IT'S *DANGEROUS* TO GET SO CLOSE?

FATHER!

GENJI? OH, NO!

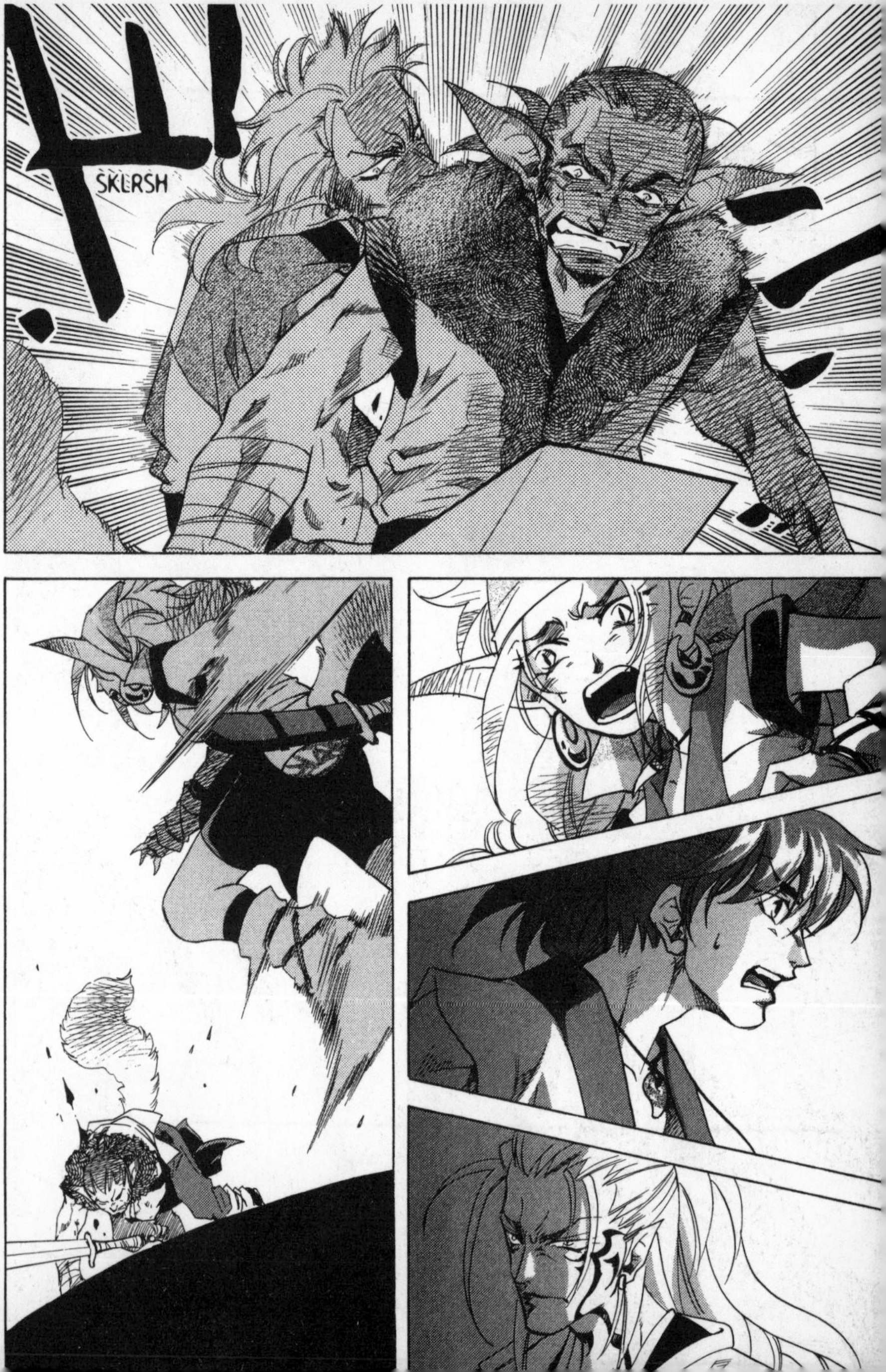
SKLRSH

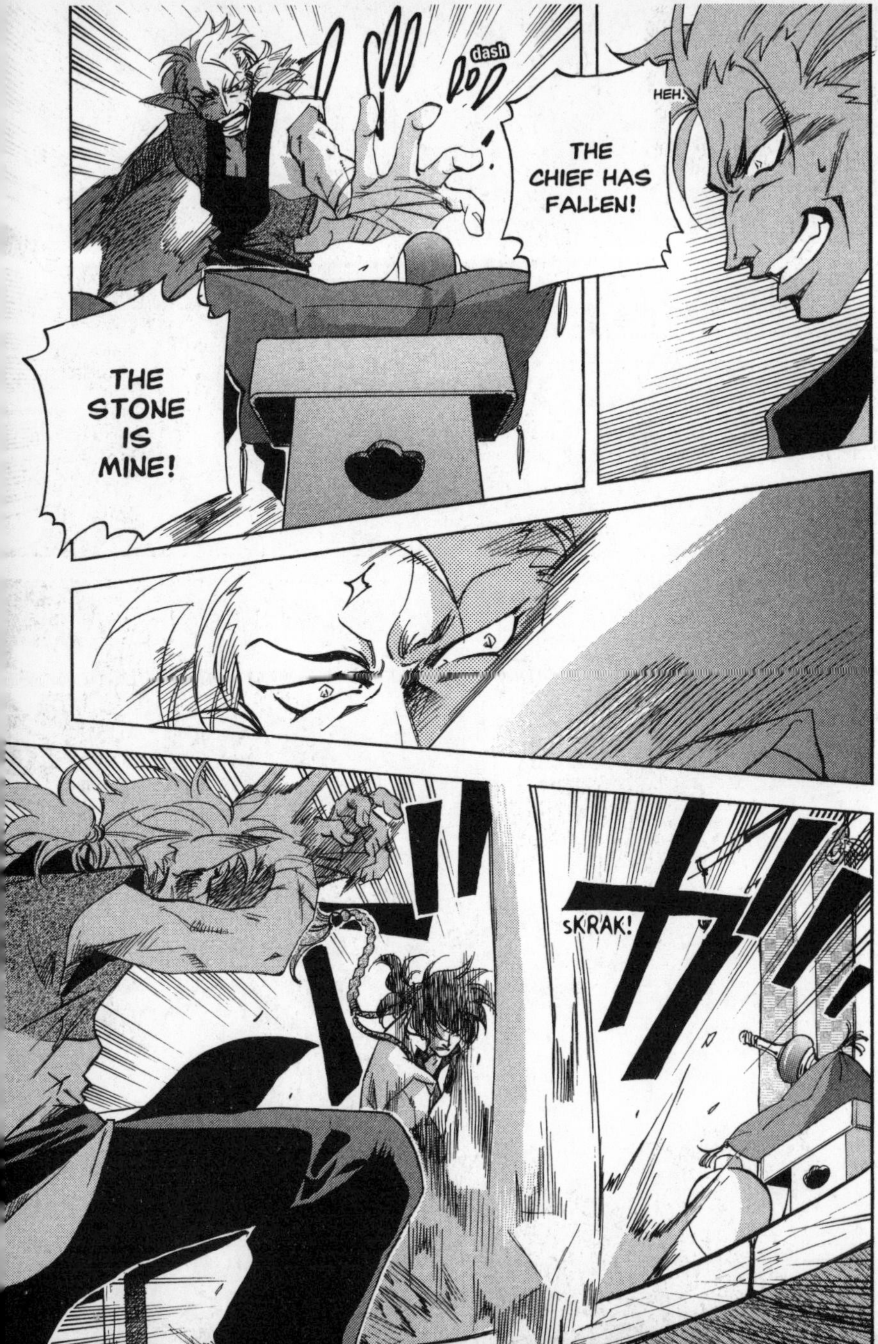
dash
THE CHIEF HAS FALLEN!
HEH.
THE STONE IS MINE!
SKRAK!

YOU'RE DEAD!

BWSH!

DROP YOUR SPEAR AND BACK AWAY FROM THE STONE! NOW!

DASH

THUD

OUT OF THE WAY!

AIEE!

STOP
IT!

IT'S
ONE DIRTY
MOVE AFTER
ANOTHER
WITH YOU,
ISN'T IT?

Jeez!

GENJI,
YOU
SON
OF A...

SHUT
UP
AND
MOVE!

GRARGH!

-SGRAK-

thp

bwsh

TNK

SUOH!
GET THE
STONE!

dash

SHWP!!

ON MY SPEAR? HOW AM I SUPPOSED TO DO THAT?!

SUOH!

DON'T LET HIM GET AWAY! QUICK, PUT THE STONE ON YOUR SPEAR!

GLARE

YOU'RE NOT GOIN' ANYWHERE!

BWOOF

WAUGH!

VGORR

WHAT THE?!

A-HA!

KA-CHK

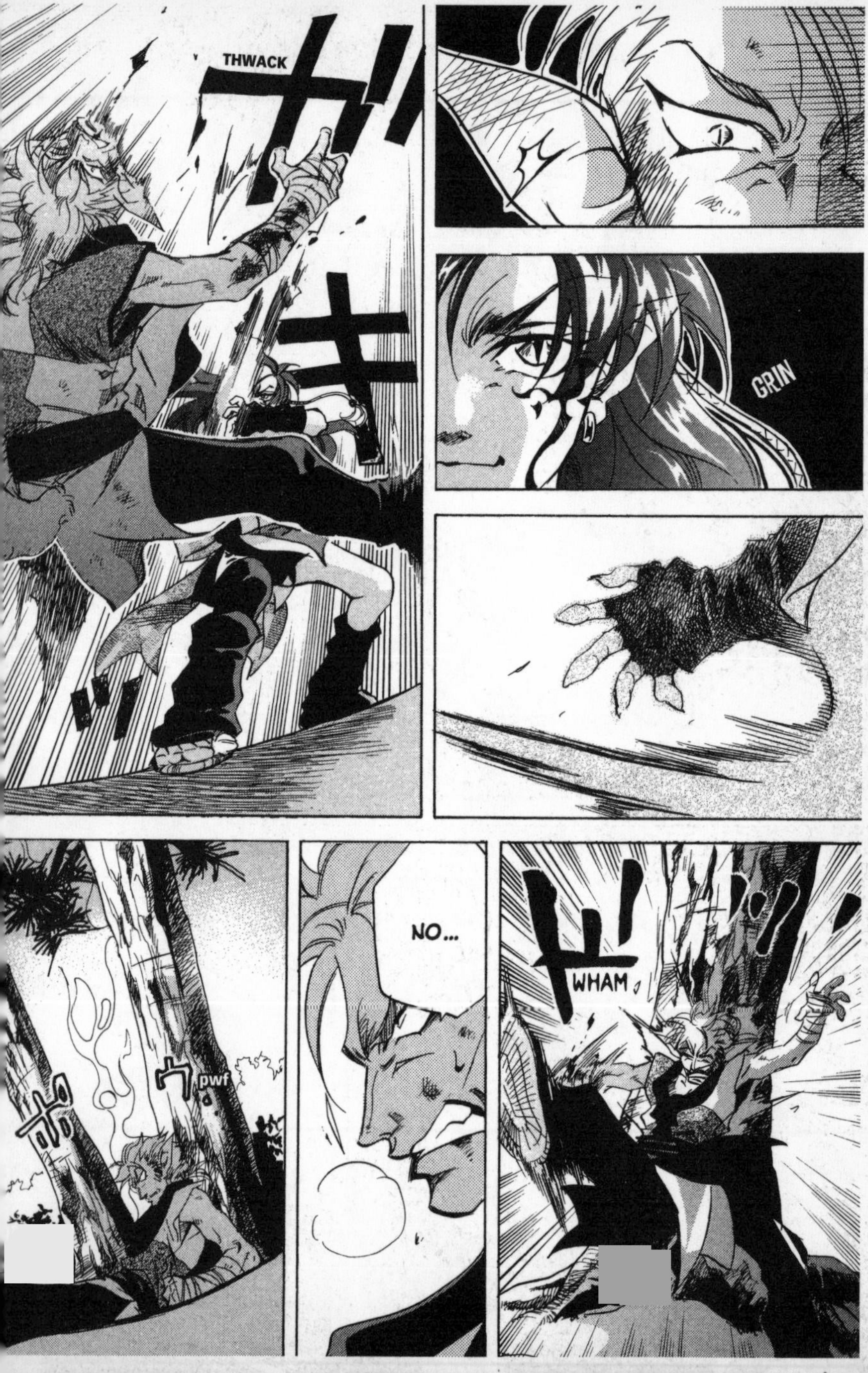
GRIN
THWACK
WHAM
NO...
pwf

DON'T LET IT GET AWAY!

LOOK! HIS DEMON ORB!

DON'T MIND IF I DO.

USE THE STONE, SUOH!

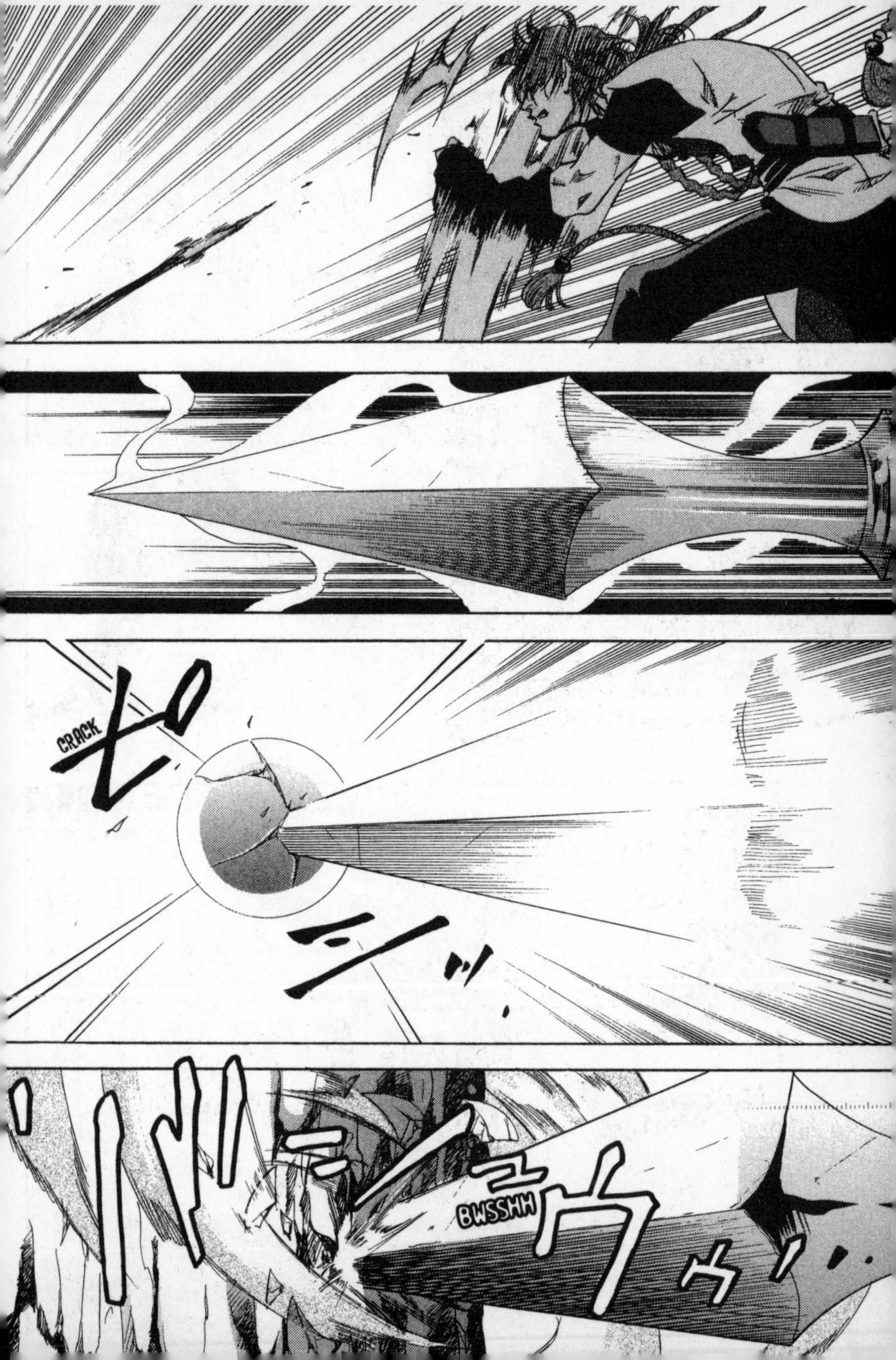
CRACK
BWSSHH

≡PHEW≡

IT'LL TAKE MORE THAN **THIS** TO GET THE BETTER OF ME.

FATHER! ARE YOU ALRIGHT?

SWSH.

SO, I GUESS WE'LL HAVE TO WAIT UNTIL YOU'RE HEALED BEFORE WE HAVE ANOTHER MATCH.

YEAH.

LOOKS LIKE IT.

WHAT? BUT...

TELL YOU WHAT, THOUGH. WHY DON'T YOU HOLD ONTO THE STONE? IT'LL BE SAFE WITH YOU.

I LIKE YOU, SUOH. WHAT DO YOU SAY NEXT TIME, WE GET TOGETHER FOR A DRINK FIRST?

HEH. YOU GOT IT.

GRIN

ANYONE WHO FEEDS US IS NICE.

YOU CAN'T GO DECIDING WHETHER SOMEONE'S "NICE" OR NOT BASED ON HOW MUCH **FOOD** THEY GIVE YOU!

JEEZ!

AND THEY PACKED US SUCH A BIG LUNCH!

THEY SURE WERE NICE, HUH?

BY THE WAY, WHY ARE YOU FOLLOWING US...

CUT IT OUT.

THAT'S WHY I ATE SO MUCH!

HEY, WE THOUGHT IT WAS ON YOU!

YOU GUYS ATE LIKE PIGS ON MY COIN!

I'M NOT LEAVIN' UNTIL I GET WHAT I'M OWED. REMEMBER LUNCH?

WHAT?!

WHEN DID I EVER SAY THAT IT WAS "ON ME"?!

THEY DID, YES.

CUT THAT OUT!

HE IS CHEAPSKATE, YES?

WELL GUESS WHAT-- UNTIL I GET MY MONEY BACK, I'M NOT GOING ANYWHERE.

SUOH?

AND YOUR MIDGET.

HUH?

squeeze

AIEE!

I SAY NOTHING!

GRAB

WHAT'D YOU SAY?!

AOI?!

(ASAGI SPEAKING)

YUP! JUST LEAVE EVERY-THING TO ME!

YEAH, BUT... ARE YOU SURE YOU'RE OK WITH THIS?

IF I'M THERE, THINGS'LL GO SMOOTHER, TOO.

AS THANKS FOR YOUR HELP, MY FATHER WANTS ME TO TAKE YOU DIRECTLY TO SAIGA.

I'M GOING WITH YOU TO IZUMO.

WHAT ARE **YOU** DOING HERE?

EXCUSE ME?! I HAVE A NAME, Y'KNOW!

HEY, YOU OVER THERE.

EEP! SHE'S ASKING FOR IT...

WHY DON'T YOU BUTT OUT?! IT'S GOT NOTHIN' TO DO WITH YOU!

GRARR

THAT SHOULD BE PLENTY.

WHATEVER. WHY DON'T YOU STOP HARPING ON ASAGI AND THEM ABOUT MONEY? YOU HAVE THE STONE, ALRIGHT?

OH, SURE! AND I'M JUST **DYIN'** TO HAVE YOU AROUND, YOU MANGY OLD MUTT!

WHAT'D YOU SAY?!

YES, IT DOES! IT'S BAD ENOUGH I HAVE TO TRAVEL WITH YOU WITH-OUT HEARING YOU RUN YOUR MOUTH ALL THE TIME!

I'VE GOT A BETTER IDEA—WHY DON'T **YOU** GO BACK TO WHATEVER JUNGLE YOU CAME SWINGING OUT OF!

STUPID APE!

JEEZ.

ENOUGH ALREADY.

Hey, I'VE ALWAYS LOOKED LIKE THIS! WHY DON'T YOU JUST GO BACK TO YOUR LITTLE VILLAGE ALREADY?

WHO'RE YOU CALLIN' AN APE?!

WHAT'D YOU SAY, DOGFACE?

YOU SURE YOU'RE NOT REALLY A FOX OR SOMETHING?

"MUTT"?! I'M A **WOLF**, YOU HALF-WIT! Y'KNOW, YOU'VE GOT A PRETTY SINISTER LOOK ABOUT YOU FOR A HUMAN!

YOU JUST TRY IT!

I'M ABOUT TO PUT WOLF ON THE MENU, GIRL!

UH, LET'S TRY WAITING A LITTLE LONGER, KAEDE.

WHAT?! SHE JUST HAD BREAKFAST!

HEY, CAN WE EAT LUNCH NOW?

YOU NEVER LEARN, DO YOU?!

CHAPTER 2: AOI / THE END

100

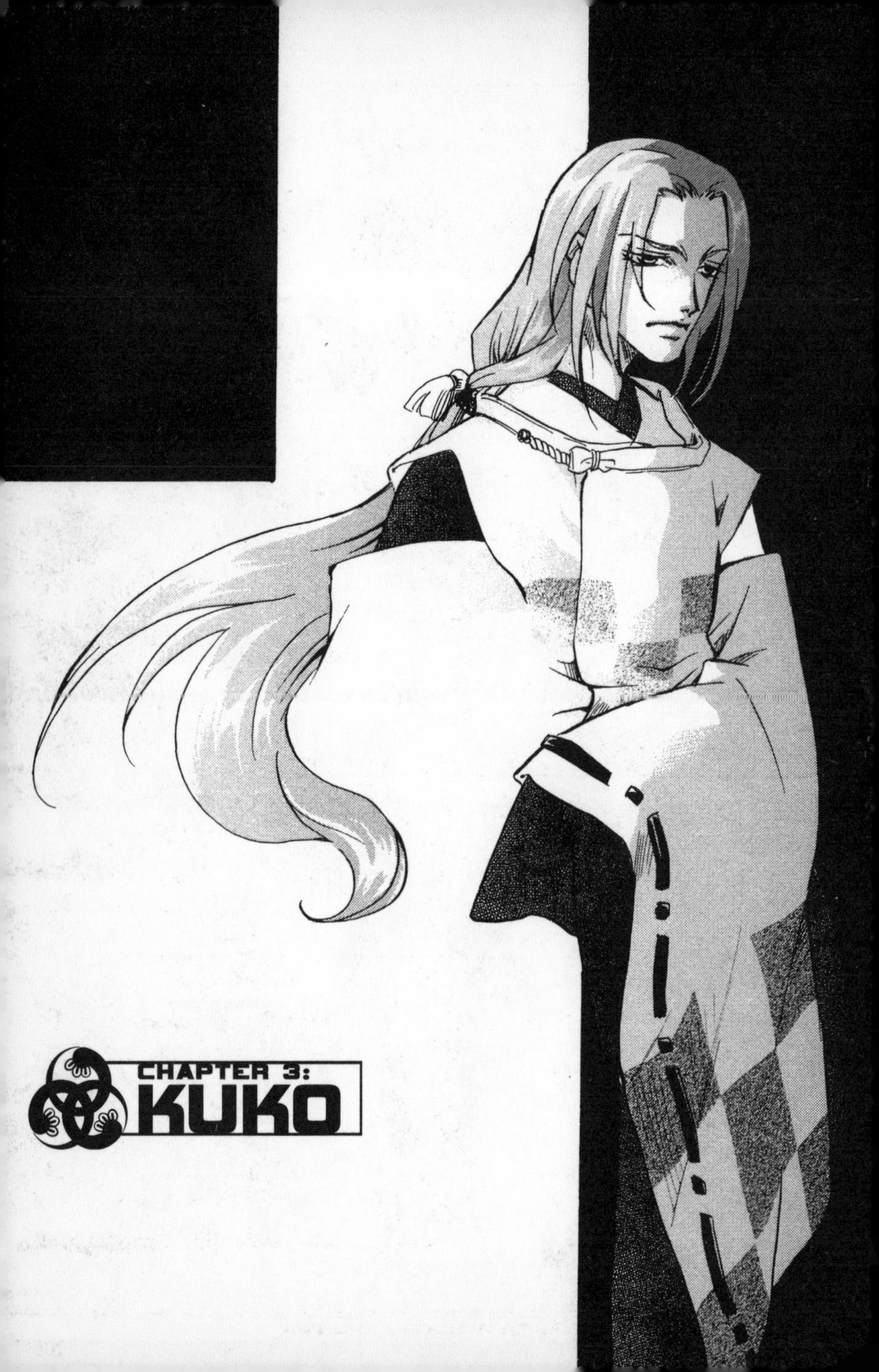
CHAPTER 3:
KUKO

SPLSSH

BLEH.

I MEAN, YOU ARE A GIRL.

YOU HAVE TO BATHE YOURSELF, KAEDE!

HOLD STILL, WILL YOU?!

AIEE!

staare

EEEK!

SQUEEZE

102

GAH!

UH...WELL, THEY'RE NOT SMALL.

But they're not that big, either.

WOULD YOU SAY YOUR BREASTS ARE BIG?

WH-WHAT DO YOU THINK YOU'RE DOING?!

WHAT?! R-REALLY?

ASAGI LIKES BIG BREASTS.

YOU TRYIN' TO START A FIGHT?

UH, SORRY TO BREAK IT TO YOU, BUT MINE ARE A LITTLE BIGGER.

MINE ARE THE SAME AS YOURS, TOO!

I'M TELLING YOU, BREASTS ARE BREASTS!

THEY'RE ALL THE SAME!

THEY WERE BIGGER THAN YOURS, BUT THE SAME AS YOURS?

THAT DOESN'T MAKE SENSE!

HE WAS ALL CHECKING 'EM OUT.

UH-HUH. THERE WAS THIS MERMAID NAMED MIZUKI. HE LIKED HER BECAUSE SHE HAD BIG BREASTS. MINE ARE THE SAME AS HERS, YOU KNOW! BUT STILL...

JEALOUS MUCH?

MIZUKI

STARE

I'D SAY THEIR BOOBS ARE THE LEAST OF THEIR PROBLEMS. Anyway, you seen one, you seen 'em all.

IT'S EMBAR-RASSING.

I WISH THEY'D STOP GOIN' ON ABOUT THEIR BOOBS.

I'M JEALOUS. WELL, AREN'T **YOU** THE LADIES' MAN!

WHAT'S THAT?

IT'S NOT A TATTOO. IT'S A **SIGIL.**

HEY KURENAI, DOES THAT TATTOO COVER YOUR WHOLE BODY?

WELL, I GUESS IT'S KIND OF LIKE A TATTOO. AS YOUR DEMONIC POWERS INCREASE, YOU GET TO ETCH MORE OF THE PATTERN ONTO YOUR BODY.

GETTING IT CAN DOUBLE YOUR STRENGTH. BUT THE PATTERN ITSELF DEPENDS ON YOUR KIND OF POWER, AND YOU ONLY GET TO CHOOSE ONE DESIGN.

DOES IT DO ANYTHING?

OH. SO MOM'S WOULD BE ICE, RIGHT?

(ASAGI SPEAKING)

MINE IS THE FLAME SIGIL.

RIGHT. AND YOUR GRANDPA HAS THE THUNDER SIGIL.

gaaze

staare

YOU'VE GOT IT ON YOUR BACK, TOO, RIGHT?

ENOUGH ALREADY! I DON'T LIKE GUYS CHECKIN' ME OUT LIKE THAT!

HUH. SO THE BIGGER AND MORE COMPLICATED YOUR SIGIL IS,

THE STRONGER YOU ARE.

C'MON, SHOW US A LITTLE MORE!

SHUT UP!

I WANT A SIGIL, TOO!

DO YOU HAVE IT ON, LIKE, THE SOLES OF YOUR FEET, TOO?

QUIT PAWIN' AT ME ALREADY!

OH, COME ON. WHAT'S THE BIG DEAL?

KAEDE?

I THINK YOUR FATHER'S BEING ATTACKED, KAEDE.

THE GUYS ARE ACTING KINDA WEIRD.

SPLSH

SPLSH

YOU ALRIGHT?

Did you find something?

IT'S AN ENCHANTMENT. THIS PARTICULAR ONE IS FOR BINDING.

SEE THAT ROCK? THERE'S SOMETHING ON IT.

I GUESS THIS MEANS THERE'S SOMETHING IN THERE.

KAEDE...

OK.

COME ON. IT'S TIME TO GET DRESSED.

WE SHOULD SHOW THIS TO THE OTHERS.

FWP

SPLSH

?

!?!

KAEDE.
THE
SEAL.

RELEASE
ME...

Huh?
KAEDE?!

NO!
DON'T
TOUCH
THAT!

SKrakk

BWSSSH

GRAUGH!

WH-WHAT WAS THAT?!

109

AOI!

I DON'T KNOW. IT'S LIKE THE LIGHT JUST SWALLOWED HER UP.

WHERE IS SHE?

I-I DON'T KNOW.

WHAT HAPPENED?! WHAT WAS THAT LIGHT?

THERE WAS AN ENCHANTMENT ON ONE OF THE ROCKS. KAEDE TORE IT OFF, AND THAT'S WHEN THAT FLASH OF LIGHT--

ASAGI! OVER THERE!

KAEDE?

SURE LOOKS LIKE HER!

HUH? BUT...

THAT'S NOT KAEDE.

WILL YOU IDIOTS CUT IT OUT? WE HAVE A BIGGER PROBLEM HERE.

HEY! WHY DO **YOU** GET TO LOOK?

It's not like looking's gonna do any harm.

GRARR

TURN YOUR HEAD.

SUOH! QUIT GAWKIN' ALREADY!

glare

111

IT'S HER BODY, BUT SHE'S BEEN **POSSESSED.**

WHO ARE YOU?

I AM A *KUKO,* A FOX SPIRIT.

YOU'RE A FAST LEARNER. THAT MAKES THINGS EASIER FOR ME, DEMON OF THE FLAME.

MY NAME IS RINDO.

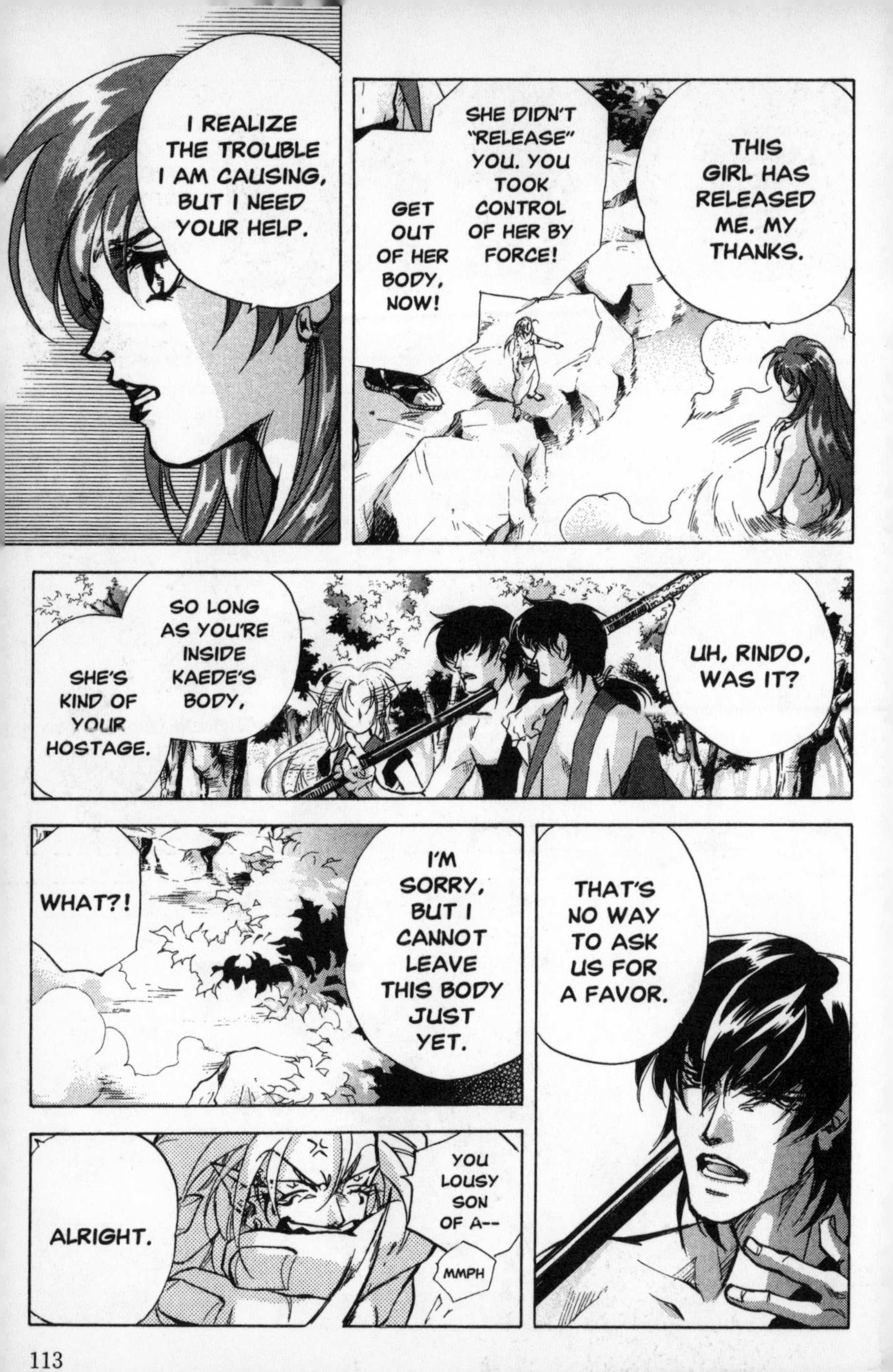
THIS GIRL HAS RELEASED ME. MY THANKS.
SHE DIDN'T "RELEASE" YOU. YOU TOOK CONTROL OF HER BY FORCE!
GET OUT OF HER BODY, NOW!
I REALIZE THE TROUBLE I AM CAUSING, BUT I NEED YOUR HELP.
UH, RINDO, WAS IT?
SO LONG AS YOU'RE INSIDE KAEDE'S BODY,
SHE'S KIND OF YOUR HOSTAGE.
THAT'S NO WAY TO ASK US FOR A FAVOR.
I'M SORRY, BUT I CANNOT LEAVE THIS BODY JUST YET.
WHAT?!
YOU LOUSY SON OF A--
MMPH
ALRIGHT.

THEN WE'LL GIVE YOU AN ANSWER.

YOU SOUND LIKE YOU HAVE YOUR REASONS FOR DOING THIS. LET'S HEAR 'EM.

GRRGH URGH URGH

YEAH, WHAT HARM COULD IT DO?

HE'S RIGHT. IF WE LISTEN TO HIS STORY, WE MIGHT FIND A WAY TO GET HIM OUT OF KAEDE.

GET IT?

I HEAR THAT *KUKO* ARE PRETTY HONEST. HE PROBABLY WON'T TRY ANYTHING FUNNY.

CALM DOWN.

ASAGI!

PWHA!

FINE!

NOW THEN. JUST OUTSIDE A VILLAGE ACROSS THE MOUNTAINS FROM HERE,

THERE LIVED AN ARISTOCRAT BY THE NAME OF ASANO.

ASANO, WHO HAD A WEAK CONSTITUTION, CHOSE TO REST THERE BECAUSE THE AIR WAS REPORTED TO BE PURE AND CLEAN.

HE LED A LONELY LIFE.

IT WAS FAR FROM THE CAPITAL, SO FEW FRIENDS VISITED, AND HIS OWN CONDITION KEPT HIM FROM LEAVING.

THAT WAS WHEN I MET HIM.

HNGH...

YOU THERE. ARE YOU ALRIGHT?!

I WAS BADLY HURT.

I WAS ATTACKED BY A BANDIT.

WHAT HAPPENED? THESE WOUNDS ARE TERRIBLE.

WAIT.

SOMEONE! THIS PERSON IS WOUNDED! HE NEEDS HELP, NOW!

MAY I REST HERE... JUST FOR A LITTLE WHILE?

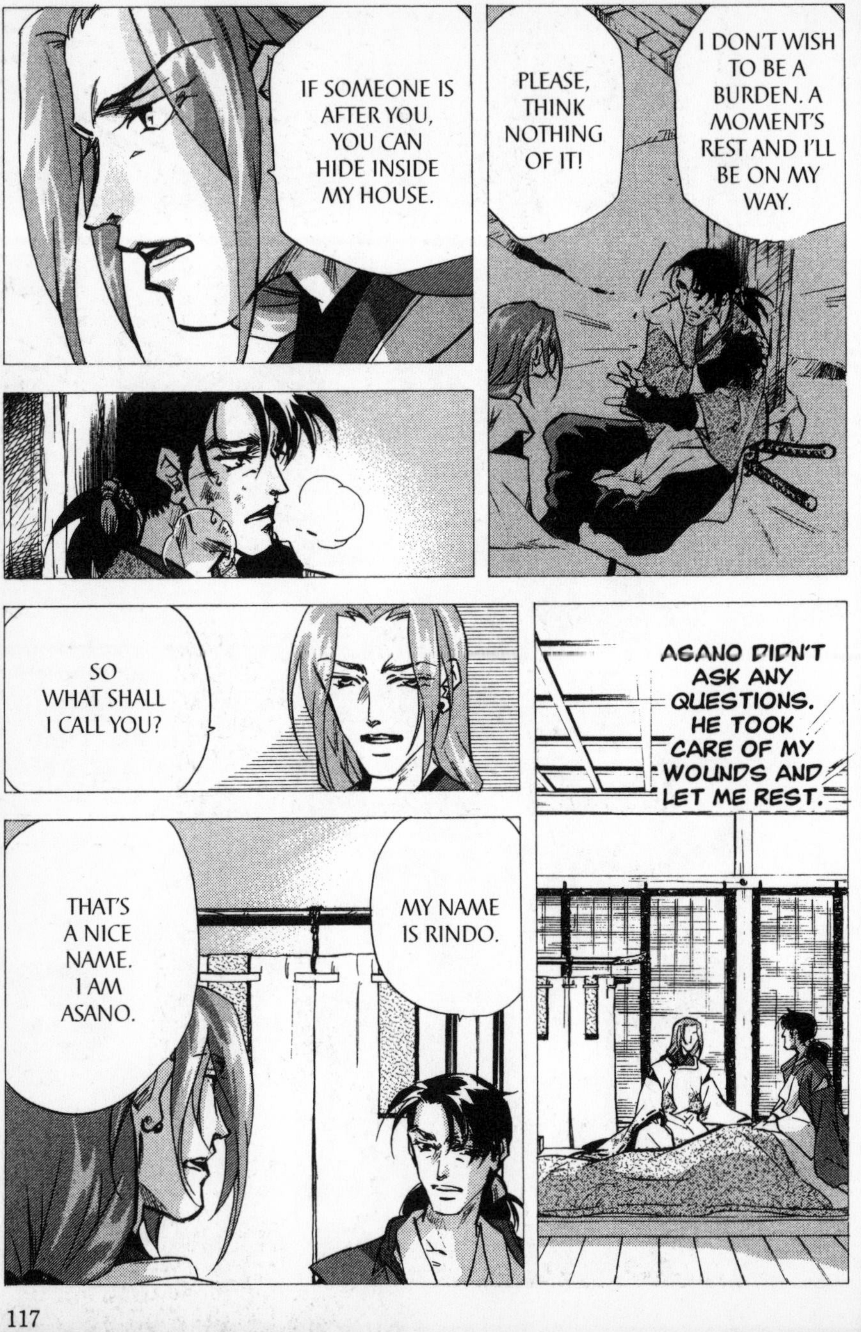
IF SOMEONE IS AFTER YOU, YOU CAN HIDE INSIDE MY HOUSE.
I DON'T WISH TO BE A BURDEN. A MOMENT'S REST AND I'LL BE ON MY WAY.
PLEASE, THINK NOTHING OF IT!
SO WHAT SHALL I CALL YOU?
MY NAME IS RINDO.
THAT'S A NICE NAME. I AM ASANO.
ASANO DIDN'T ASK ANY QUESTIONS. HE TOOK CARE OF MY WOUNDS AND LET ME REST.

AND IF YOU DON'T MIND, I WOULD ENJOY YOUR COMPANY EVERY ONCE IN A WHILE.

I LIVE ALONE, SO YOU NEED NOT WORRY. PLEASE, JUST TEND TO YOUR WOUNDS.

THAT'S VERY KIND.

WE TALKED ABOUT MANY THINGS, AND GREW TO RESPECT EACH OTHER.

BY THE TIME MY WOUNDS HEALED...

ASANO AND I HAD A LOT IN COMMON.

118

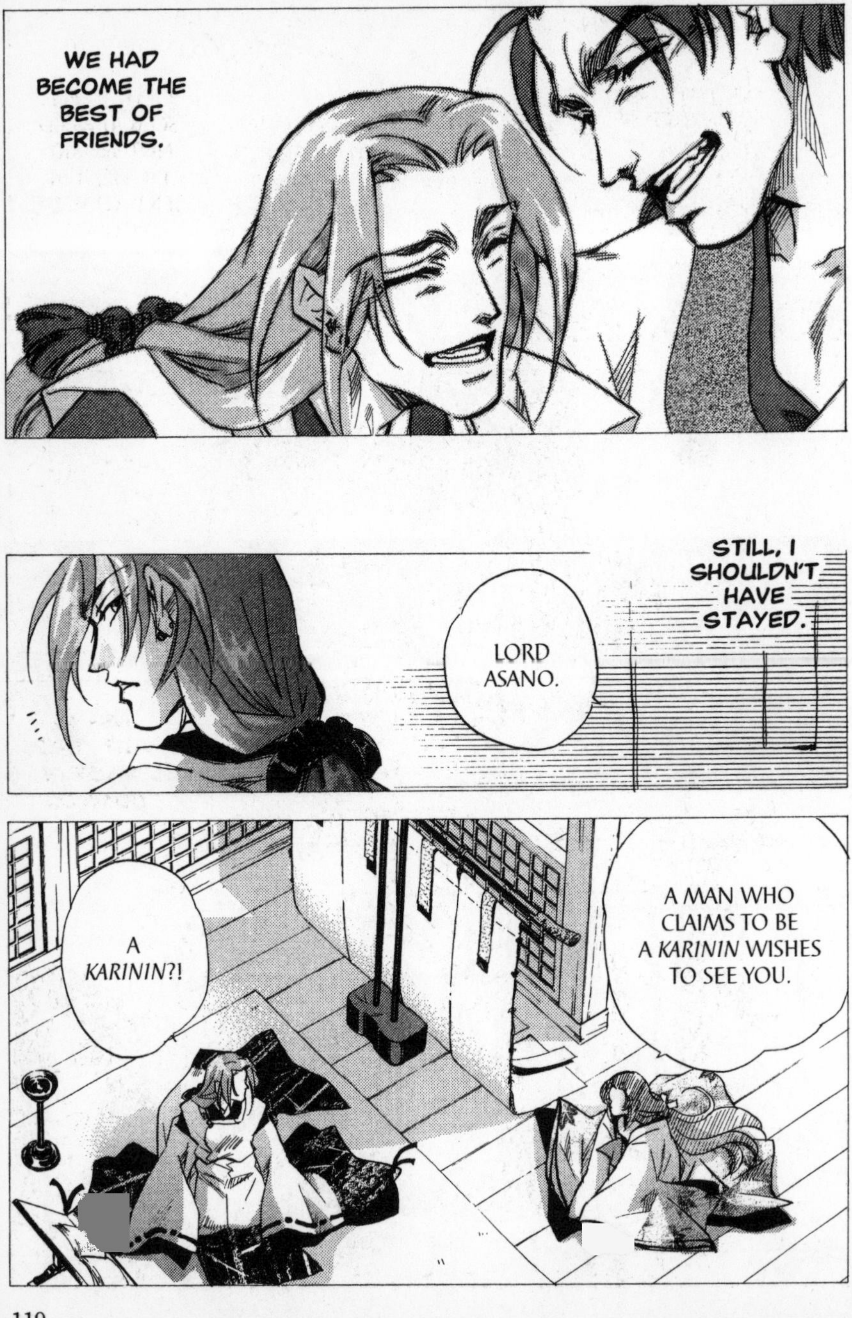
WE HAD BECOME THE BEST OF FRIENDS.
STILL, I SHOULDN'T HAVE STAYED.
LORD ASANO.
A MAN WHO CLAIMS TO BE A *KARININ* WISHES TO SEE YOU.
A *KARININ*?!

YES, BUT...

VERY WELL. I SHALL MEET WITH HIM. BUT DO NOT MENTION RINDO.

TELL HIM THAT I AM THE ONLY ONE IN THIS HOUSE. DO YOU UNDERSTAND?

MY NAME IS TSUKUMO.

IT IS AN HONOR TO MEET YOU, LORD ASANO.

INDEED. I HAVE CHASED A PARTICULAR FOX ALL THE WAY FROM NANKAI ROAD.

ARE YOU IN SEARCH OF PREY?

I HEAR THAT YOU ARE A *KARININ*.

I'VE HEARD THERE ARE TWO TYPES OF SUCH CREATURES: *ZENKO* AND *YAKO*.

ZENKO ARE PEACEFUL, WHILE--

IRRELEVANT.

IT IS A CUNNING BEAST THAT HAS DISGUISED ITSELF AS A MAN.

YOU DON'T SAY.

ALL DEMONS DESERVE DEATH.

THAT'S NOT WHAT I MEANT.

HA HA! DON'T TELL ME THAT YOU WOULD SIDE WITH DEMONS, LORD ASANO.

THAT'S A RATHER HARSH WAY OF THINKING.

BY THE WAY, HAVE YOU SEEN THE FOX I'M AFTER?

NO. I HAVEN'T SEEN ANYONE LIKE THAT.

HE SHOULD BE SEVERELY WOUNDED.

THAT WOULD BE APPRECIATED.

IF I HEAR ANYTHING, I WILL LET YOU KNOW.

WE ARE FAR FROM THE VILLAGE, AND I AM THE ONLY PERSON TO BE FOUND FOR MILES.

WE WILL MEET AGAIN AGAIN.

GRIN

YOU MAY REACH ME AT THE RANGER'S OFFICE IN THE VILLAGE.

SEARCHING THIS AREA WILL TAKE SOME TIME.

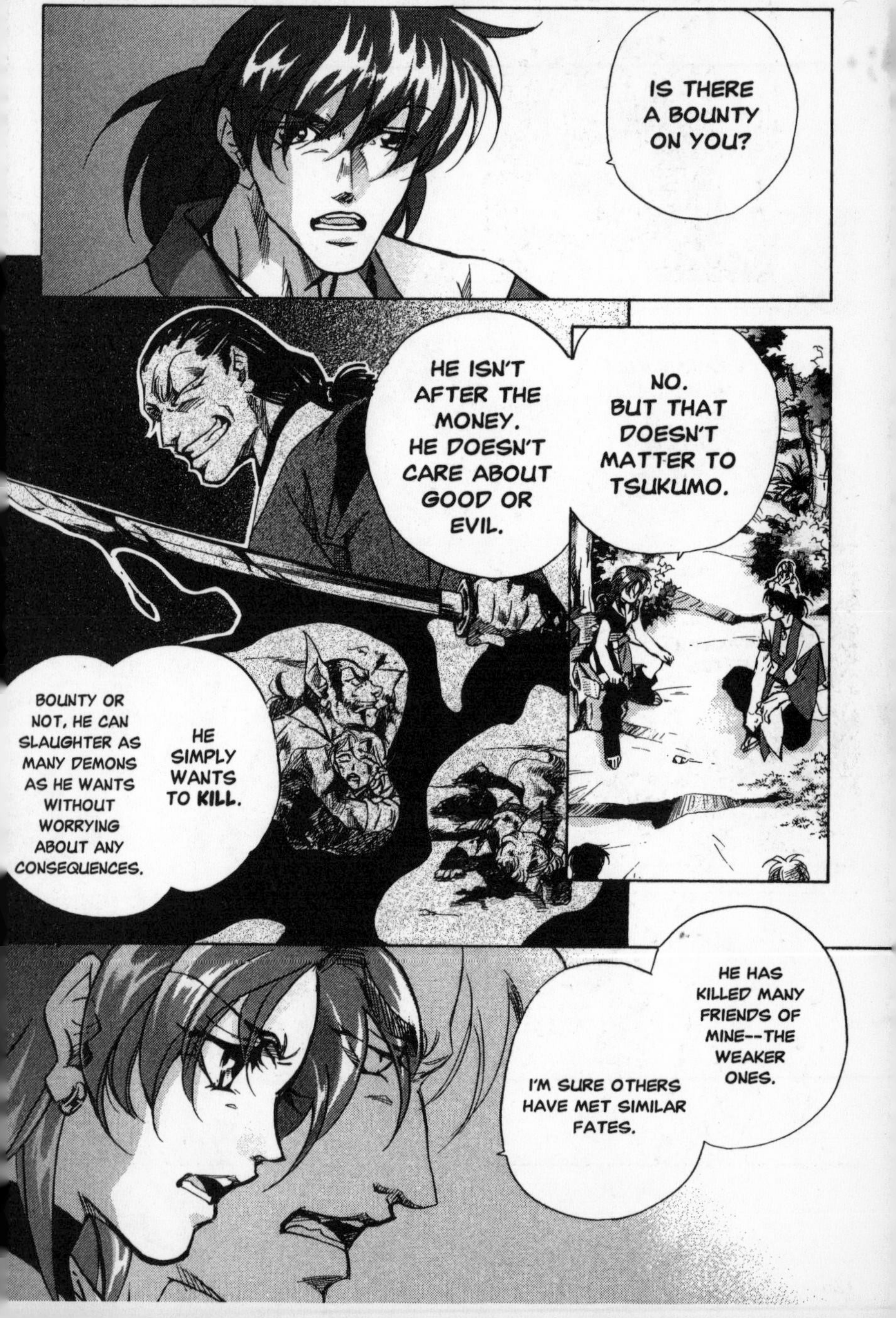
IS THERE A BOUNTY ON YOU?
NO. BUT THAT DOESN'T MATTER TO TSUKUMO.
HE ISN'T AFTER THE MONEY. HE DOESN'T CARE ABOUT GOOD OR EVIL.
HE SIMPLY WANTS TO KILL.
BOUNTY OR NOT, HE CAN SLAUGHTER AS MANY DEMONS AS HE WANTS WITHOUT WORRYING ABOUT ANY CONSEQUENCES.
HE HAS KILLED MANY FRIENDS OF MINE--THE WEAKER ONES.
I'M SURE OTHERS HAVE MET SIMILAR FATES.

I THINK HE HAD AN IDEA. THAT'S WHY HE HID ME FROM TSUKUMO.

DID THIS ASANO GUY KNOW WHAT YOU REALLY ARE?

clench

I SHOULDN'T HAVE LET HIM GET INVOLVED IN THIS.

IT CAME FROM OVER THERE!

A SCREAM?

AAUGH!

I SENSE SOMETHING...

IT'S RINDO, ISN'T IT? LET'S GO AFTER HIM!

KAEDE, WAIT!

DON'T **DO** THAT, YOU IDIOT!

dash

WHERE ARE YOU, FOX? SHOW YOURSELF!

HE WASN'T INSIDE THIS GUY.

I KNOW YOU'RE HERE. I CAN SMELL YOU!

COME OUT!

BWSH

NOOOOO!

EEK!

SO YOU'RE IN THERE, EH?

RUSTLE

N-NO!

STOP, TSUKUMO!

NO. **THAT'S** WHERE YOU ARE.

I'VE BEEN LOOKING FOR YOU.

RINDO!

KASHING

SMASH

HYAA!

BUT YOU JUST SAID IT'S TSUKUMO! *Didn't you?*

WHY NOT? THAT'S TSUKUMO, RIGHT?

WAIT! DON'T HURT HIM!

YES, BUT IT'S ASANO, TOO!

AND **THIS** IS THE RESULT!

I TOLD YOU. I GOT ASANO INVOLVED...

LEAVE? WHAT DO... HEY, SOMETHING FEELS WARM.

SHIMMER

LOOK!

OH!

dash

AAAUGH!

FWOOSH

I'M SORRY, BUT I NEED YOU TO LEAVE RIGHT NOW.

SNICKER

THAT'S FUNNY.

I PROMISE I'LL BE BACK. WAIT HERE.

HUH?

MY BODY'S TURNING INVISIBLE.

RUNNING AWAY AGAIN?

YOU CAN'T STAND TO LEAVE HIM THIS WAY.

OF COURSE YOU'LL RETURN, RINDO.

WHA...

WE'RE BACK WHERE WE WERE BEFORE. SEE, THERE'S THE HOT SPRING.

WHAT'S GOING ON? WHERE ARE WE?!

FWP

FWP

CALM DOWN.

CHK

FHOOSH

YES.

THAT THING YOU JUST DID...WAS THAT A TIME SHIFT?

HE'S THE REASON I MUST ASK FOR YOUR HELP.

ANYWAY, WHO **WAS** THAT GUY?

WOW!

HMPH.

THAT AIN'T TRUE.

ISN'T THAT A REALLY HIGH-LEVEL TECHNIQUE? MY FATHER TOLD ME THAT IT TAKES AN INCREDIBLE AMOUNT OF POWER.

SHUT UP!

BINGO

HAS THE POWER, LACKS THE SKILL

I BET YOU CAN'T DO IT, KURENAI.

Hee hee.

HMPH.

SEEMS LIKE YOU DRAGGED US BACK HERE TO EXPLAIN, BUT WE'RE NOT GONNA HELP YOU, NO MATTER...

WE HAVE ONE CONDITION.

NAME IT.

LEMME GO!

flap
flap

SQUEEZE

GAURGH!

WE'LL COOPERATE AS LONG AS YOU PROMISE TO GIVE BACK THAT GIRL YOU'VE POSSESSED, UNHARMED.

BUT IF SOMETHING HAPPENS TO KAEDE...

YOU'RE IN FOR A WORLD OF TROUBLE.

UNDER-STOOD.

THAT DAY...

ASANO DECIDED NOT TO TELL ME ABOUT TSUKUMO'S VISIT.

BUT I HAPPENED TO SEE TSUKUMO LEAVING THE HOUSE.

SO YOU REALLY ARE THE FOX HE'S LOOKING FOR.

I SEE.

I KNEW I COULDN'T KEEP MY SECRET ANY LONGER, SO I TOLD ASANO EVERYTHING.

NOW THAT TSUKUMO IS HERE, THERE IS NO WAY I CAN STAY.

BUT IT WAS TOO DIFFICULT TO BID YOU FAREWELL.

I'M SORRY. I INTENDED TO LEAVE AS SOON AS I WAS HEALED.

YOU GET THEIR BODIES AFTER THEY DIE.

I USE MY POWERS TO GIVE THEM ONE MORE YEAR. AND IN EXCHANGE...

CORRECT.

HOW LONG HAVE YOU POSSESSED THIS MAN'S BODY?

IT'S A LITTLE DIFFERENT THAN POSSESSION. WHEN HUMANS ARE ON THE BRINK OF DEATH, THEY OFTEN WISH FOR MORE TIME.

YES.

CAN YOU TELL IF SOMEONE IS GOING TO DIE SOON?

SINCE I HAVE BEEN WITH YOU, I'VE EXPERIENCED A SENSE OF PEACE I'VE NEVER KNOWN BEFORE.

THAT'S WHY I COULDN'T LEAVE YOU!

NO! OF COURSE NOT, ASANO.

IS THAT WHY YOU CAME TO ME?

WILL YOU GIVE ME ONE MORE YEAR?

I DON'T HAVE MUCH LONGER TO LIVE, DO I?

THEN I ASK YOU FOR THE TRUTH ONCE MORE.

THAT IS WHY I WANTED TO ASK YOU...

DON'T LOOK SO TROUBLED. IT'S MY BODY. I'M WELL AWARE OF MY CONDITION.

I NEVER LAUGHED. I HAD GIVEN UP HOPE, AND I THOUGHT MY LIFE WAS DESTINED TO END IN SOLITUDE.

RINDO, I HAVE HAD A LONELY LIFE IN THIS PLACE.

YES. I WILL GIVE YOU THIS BODY.

ASANO, DO YOU MEAN...

BUT...

136

I CAN'T EVEN EXPRESS HOW HAPPY YOU'VE MADE ME.

BUT THEN YOU CAME ALONG AND GAVE ME THE BEST TIMES OF MY LIFE.

ASANO...

WHERE IS YOUR FRIEND THE FOX?

EXCUSE ME, LORD ASANO.

AFTER THAT, I DECIDED TO LEAVE THE HOUSE IMMEDIATELY. I PROMISED ASANO THAT I WOULD RETURN...

NO THANKS!

I'LL GET MY MASTER.

ONE MOMENT.

BUT I SHOULD NOT HAVE LEFT.

BY THE LIKES OF YOU!

YOU HAD BETTER TELL ME, FOR YOUR OWN GOOD.

I CAN'T ALLOW

RINDO TO BE KILLED...

HA.

WHAT A JOKE!

YOU THINK YOU CAN ATTACK ME?! YOU'RE NOTHING BUT A SICKLY, DOWN-AND-OUT ARISTOCRAT.

WHAM

SKLRSSH

HOW
COULD
THIS BE?

∋PANT∈

∋GASP∈

∋PANT∈

BY THE TIME I CAME BACK TO THE HOUSE...

SHLRP

GRGHH

ASANO WAS NO LONGER HIMSELF.

I CAN'T DIE... I REFUSE TO! I HAVEN'T HAD ENOUGH... I WANT MORE!

MORE BLOOD, MORE SCREAMS... FROM THOSE DEMONS.

TSUKUMO'S EVIL ESSENCE TRANSFORMED HIM INTO SOMETHING INHUMAN.

A HUMAN POSSESSED BY ANOTHER HUMAN?! HOW'S THAT EVEN POSSIBLE?

COULD THAT REALLY BE TRUE?

THEY SAY MEN ARE CAPABLE OF BECOMING MONSTERS IF THEIR HEARTS ARE EVIL ENOUGH.

HAVING NO CHOICE, I SEALED MY AURA IN THAT ROCK FORMATION.

I WAS ATTACKED BY BANDITS AND LOST MY BODY.

I COULDN'T BEAR TO HARM ASANO, SO I ESCAPED. BUT WHEN I GOT HERE,

BUT I COULDN'T FREE MYSELF OF THIS SPELL.

YES. I SUPPRESSED MY PRESENCE TO HIDE FROM TSUKUMO.

SO YOU DID THAT BY YOURSELF?

That charm?

AND THIS GIRL JUST HAPPENED TO HAVE THE QUALITIES OF A MEDIUM.

THAT'S WHEN YOU APPEARED.

SO YOU DECIDED TO "BORROW" HER?

WHAT'S A MEDIUM?

141

 BUT HOW ARE WE GOING TO GET THIS TSUKUMO GUY TO LEAVE ASANO'S BODY?

 KAEDE IS EASILY POSSESSED. HER MOTHER WAS A SHRINE MAIDEN, SO I GUESS THAT HAS SOMETHING TO DO WITH IT.

 THAT DEPENDS ON YOU, AND YOUR POWER.

 OUR POWER?

142

YOU'LL HAVE TO KILL ME FIRST.

HA!

YOU CAME BACK. WHAT A STUPID, LOYAL FOX YOU ARE.

I'M TAKING ASANO BACK.

YOU CAN'T HARM THIS BODY!

chk

RIP

FOR YOU TO KILL ME.

IT WILL BE EASY FOR ME TO KILL YOU. BUT NOT SO EASY...

!!

DASH

ISN'T THAT RIGHT, RINDO?!

STOP!!

SLASH

GRRGH!!

BSKRK

WE ONLY HAVE ONE CHANCE-- PLACE AN ENCHANTMENT OF IMMOBILIZATION ON HIM, THEN...

YES. IF WE DO THAT, WE CAN GET TSUKUMO OUT OF ASANO'S BODY.

WHAT?! YOU WANT ME TO STAB IT?

MOST WEAPONS CANNOT CUT MY CHARMS, BUT THAT SWORD OF YOURS HAS EXTRAORDINARY POWERS.

YOU SHOULD BE ABLE TO CUT THROUGH BOTH THE CHARM AND TSUKUMO.

KILL TSUKUMO!

BUT WHAT ABOUT ASANO?!

HE'LL BE FINE. THE CHARM WILL ABSORB THE DAMAGE.

PLEASE, ASAGI...

VWOOSH

YAAAH!

SUOH!
HE'S
OUT!
SUOH!

ZWORR

GRGH!

GRAARH

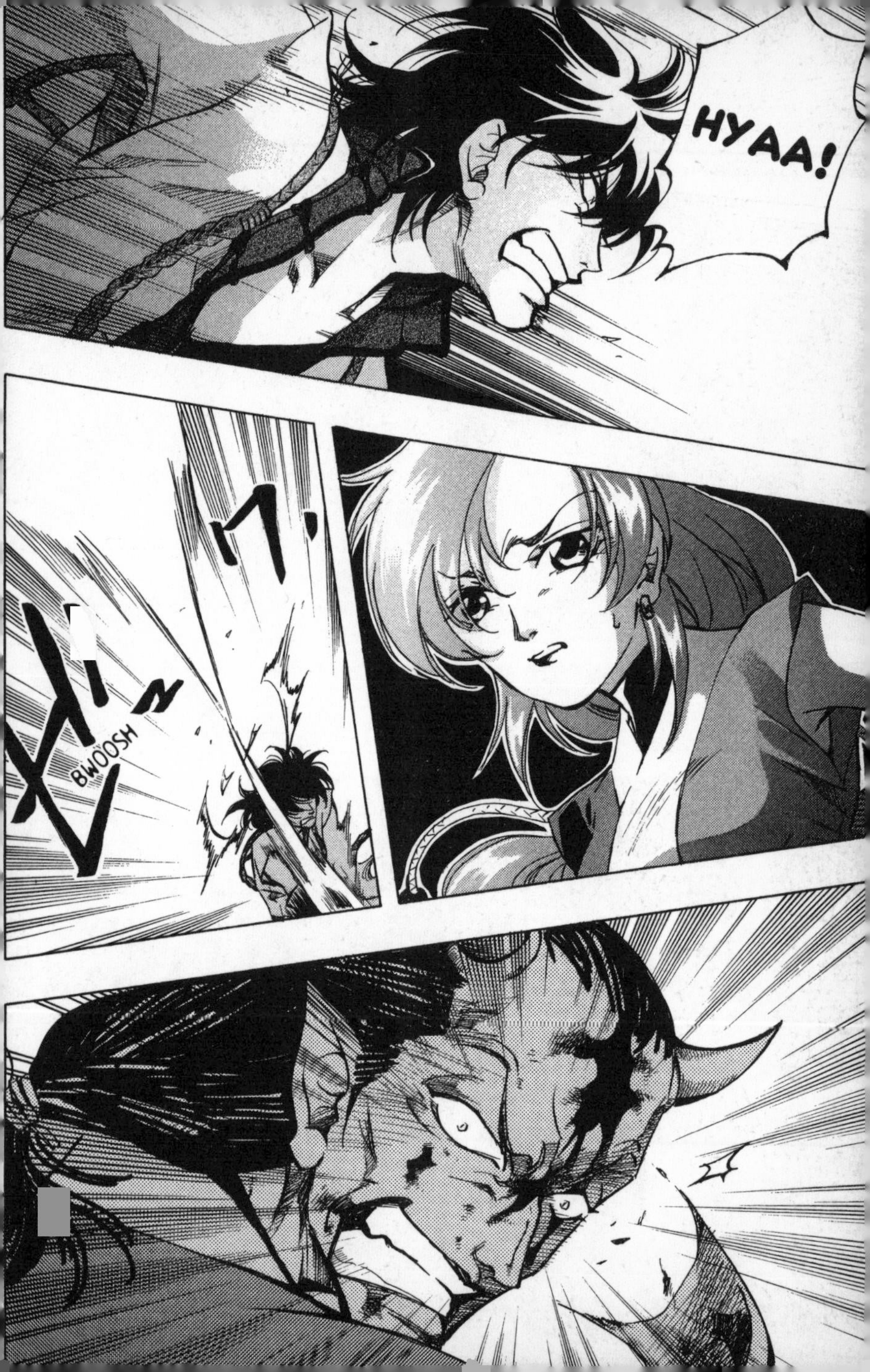
HYAA!
BWOOSH

SKRAK

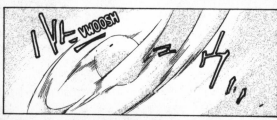

VHOOSH

SHIMMER

ZZZ

HARD
TO TELL.

HOW
IS
HE?

YES.

SO I PRESS THIS STONE AGAINST YOUR FORE-HEAD?

silence

tap

HERE GOES.

SHIMMER

WAUGH!

AAAAA!

DAZED

WHERE? UH...

GRUMBLE

ASAGI? WHERE ARE WE?

KAEDE? DO YOU RECOGNIZE ME?

I'M HUNGRY.

When are we gonna eat?

HERE YOU GO.

THE NEXT DAY

THANK YOU.

HEH.

SQUEEZE

OOOW!

CAN'T... BREATHE...

LUCKY YOU, KAEDE.

YAY! SHE'S BACK TO NORMAL!

I'll give you some food!

GET YOUR HANDS OFF HER!

THANKS. WE'LL DO THAT.

PLEASE COME VISIT ME WHEN YOUR TASKS ARE COMPLETE.

I AM IN YOUR DEBT.

DON'T WORRY ABOUT IT. AFTER ALL, WE GOT KAEDE BACK UNHARMED.

I THANK YOU AS WELL, AND I PROMISE TO RETURN THIS FAVOR SOMEDAY.

HAVE A SAFE JOURNEY.

BUT HE'LL BE STUCK IN THAT STONE FOR A WHILE.

WHAT'RE YOU SAYING THAT FOR? IF HE WANTS TO RETURN THE FAVOR, LET HIM DO IT.

THANKS. TAKE CARE OF YOURSELVES, TOO.

YOU REALLY DON'T REMEMBER A THING, DO YOU?

HMM.

SPOOKY.

THE STONE'S TALKING!

BUT THOSE TWO WILL SPEND THE REST OF THEIR TIME TOGETHER IN LAUGHTER.

GOODBYE!

YEAH.

I GUESS RINDO WILL BE ALL ALONE ONCE ASANO DIES.

I'M SURE OF IT.

CHAPTER 3: KUKO / THE END

CLAP

THANKS
FOR THE
MEAL!

HUH?!

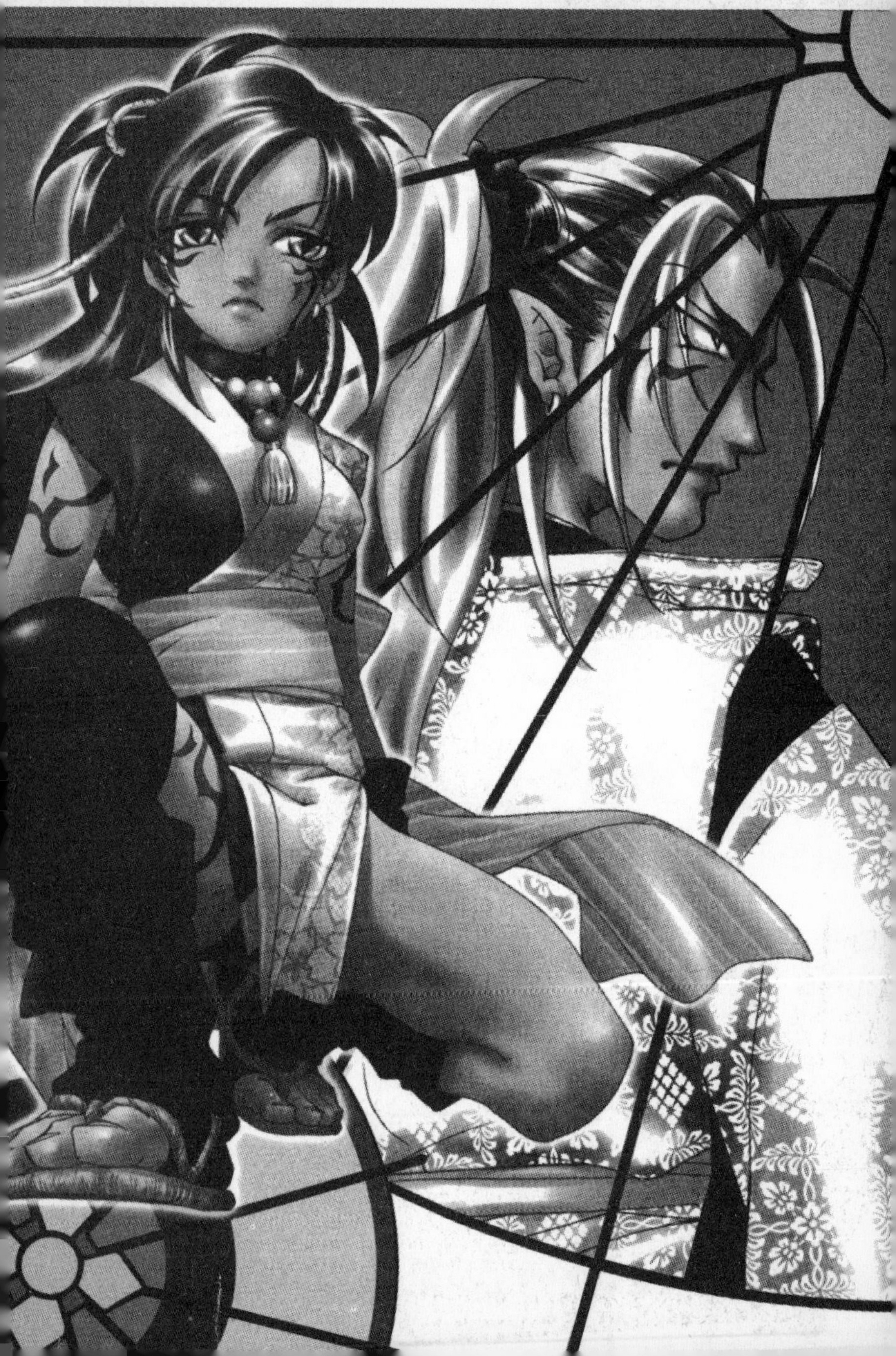

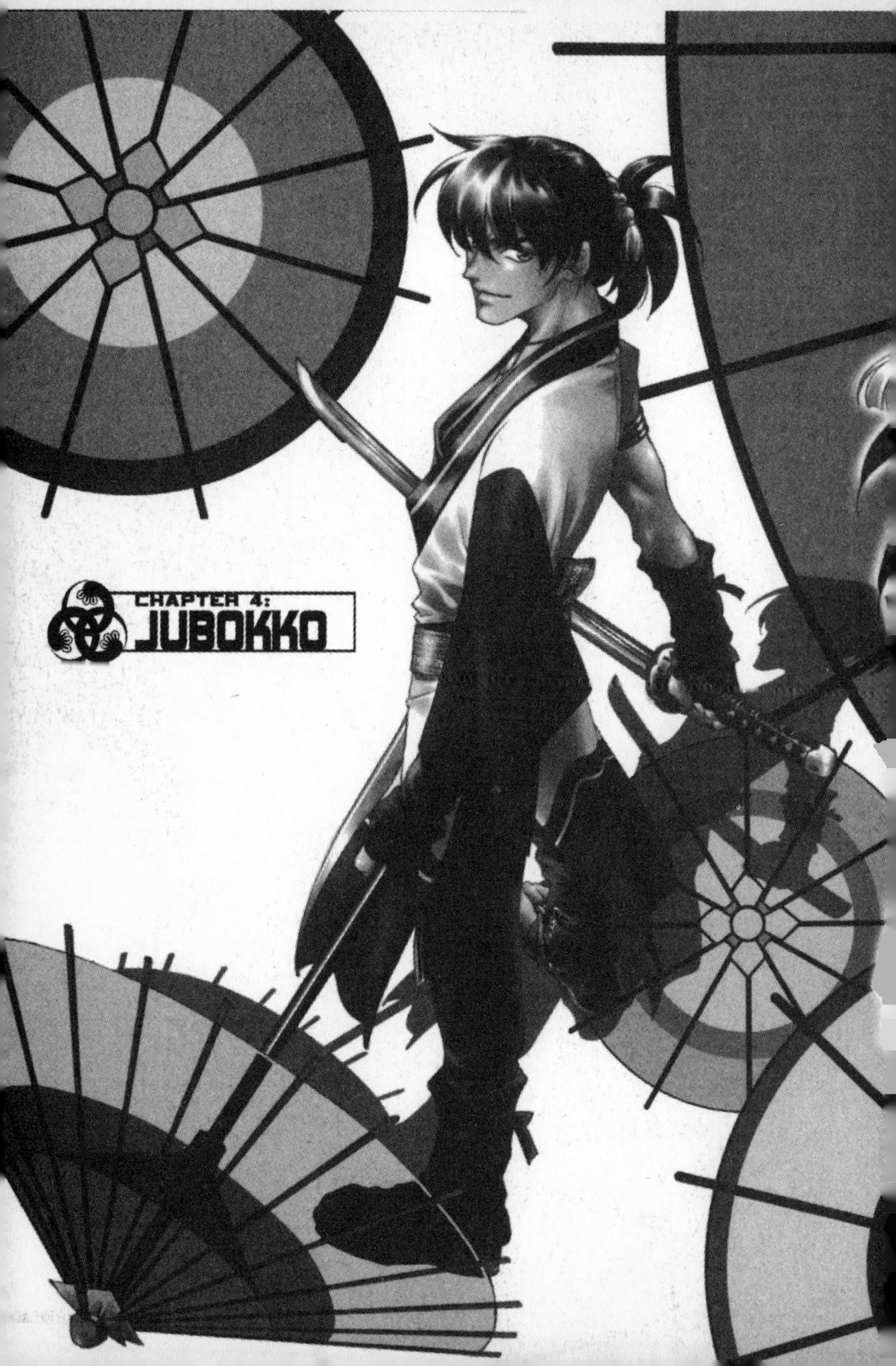
CHAPTER 4:
JUBOKKO

BY THE SWORD

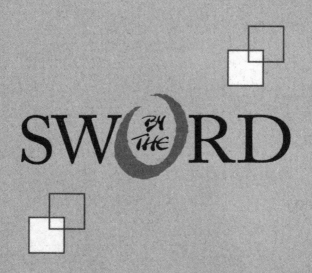

YOU PICKED UP SOMETHING WEIRD AND ATE IT, DIDN'T YOU?

SPIT IT UP.

YOU USUALLY EAT AT LEAST TEN!

IT'S STRANGE TO SEE YOU STOP AT JUST TWO SERVINGS.

ARE YOU SICK, KAEDE?

OH DEAR...

WHAT HAPPENED?

IS IT CONSTIPATION? DIARRHEA?

HOW RUDE! THERE'S NOTHING WRONG WITH ME.

GRRR

ƎGASPƐ

SOME-THING MUST BE WRONG.

KAEDE ACTUALLY SOUNDS SENSIBLE.

CRUNCH CRUNCH

MUNCH CRUNCH

MUNCH MUNCH

HEY!

THAT'S ENOUGH, YOU GUYS.

Stop eating everything.

I'M FINE.

ARE YOU SURE YOU'RE OK?

WE'RE RUNNING OUT OF MONEY, SO IT'S JUST AS WELL.

IT'S TRUE. WE'RE RUNNING OUT OF MONEY.

SEE? THE MONEY I BROUGHT FROM HOME IS GONE, TOO.

YOU DON'T HAVE ANY OTHER SKILLS.

HELL, THAT'S THE ONLY WAY YOU *KARININ* **CAN** MAKE MONEY, ISN'T IT?

MAYBE WE SHOULD HUNT FOR SOME DEMONS.

YEAH...

PRETTY MUCH.

THE IWAMI RANGER'S OFFICE SHOULD BE CLOSE BY.

WHY YOU?

OH. IF THAT'S THE CASE, I'LL GO.

I CAN HANDLE IT. YOU GUYS WAIT HERE.

ALL WE NEED IS SOMEONE TO CHECK OUT THE BOUNTY NOTICES, RIGHT?

I GUESS YOU'RE RIGHT.

I'M A WOLF, REMEMBER? AND A PUREBLOOD AT THAT.

I'M FASTER THAN ANY OF YOU.

LEAVE IT TO ME. ♡

THANKS.

THAT'D BE GREAT, AOI.

♪ I KNOW!

YOU DIDN'T HAVE TO POINT IT OUT.

OR ELSE IT'S OBVIOUS YOU'RE NOT HUMAN.

DON'T FORGET TO HIDE THAT THING HANGING OFF YOUR ASS.

ASS

OOPS.

HEY.

WHAT?

SO...

WHAT THE HELL'RE WE SUPPOSED TO DO IN THE MIDDLE OF THE MOUNTAINS?!

HUNT DEMONS. THAT'S WHAT!

SOMEWHERE IN HERE

THERE'S A VILLAGE AT THE FOOT OF THIS MOUNTAIN,

AND THE PEOPLE WHO LIVE THERE USE THIS ROAD TO GET TO THE NEXT TOWN.

SYMBOL: "MOUNTAIN"

SHOULDN'T WE BE LOOKING FOR A MORE POPULATED AREA.

BUT AOI, DEMONS WITH BOUNTIES ON THEM USUALLY CAUSE TROUBLE IN **VILLAGES.**

DON'T WORRY. I'VE ALREADY ASKED AROUND.

THIS IS A ROAD?!

IT LOOKS MORE LIKE A DEER TRAIL!

AND DEMONS ARE RESPONSIBLE?

ANYWAY, A NUMBER OF VILLAGERS HAVE GONE MISSING AROUND HERE OVER THE PAST FEW MONTHS.

IT'S BETTER THAN NOTHING, ISN'T IT?

IS THAT ENOUGH TO FEED US?

THAT'S NOT MUCH OF A BOUNTY!

I DON'T KNOW FOR SURE...

RUSTLE

BUT THE VILLAGERS SAY THEY'VE SEEN THESE GUYS ROAMING AROUND.

FWP.

I'LL GO WITH ASAGI!

YAY! ♡

IT'S JUST A COUPLE OF PUNY DEMONS. WE SHOULD SPLIT UP.

FINE. LET'S TRY SEARCHING THIS AREA.

ASAGI WON'T BE ABLE TO USE THE MOEGI IF KAEDE'S AWAY.

YOU'RE PRETTY STUPID.

GRRR

WHAT'D YOU DO **THAT** FOR?!

I'LL KILL YOU!

うぬ

NOT SO FAST!

SLAM!

HEY, WHO ARE YOU TALKING TO? IT'S LIKE YOU'RE EXPLAINING IT TO THE READERS OR SOMETHING.

I AM.

WHEN ASAGI DRAWS THE MOEGI, KURENAI GOES INTO KAEDE'S BODY. YOU SHOULD KNOW THAT BY NOW!

IDIOT! WHAT IF SOMETHING HAPPENS AND ASAGI CAN'T FIGHT BECAUSE KAEDE ISN'T AROUND?! WHAT THEN?

STILL, IT'S NOT LIKE SHE HAS TO STAY CLOSE TO HIM EVERY SECOND OF--

FINE WITH ME.

LET'S MEET AT THE RANGER OFFICE BEFORE SUNSET.

KNOW-IT-ALL.

GIVE UP, AOI. SUOH THINK HE'S RIGHT ABOUT EVERYTHING.

OH, NO, SUOH. YOU ALWAYS RIGHT!

I'M WITH YOU 100%.

ARE YOU SAYING I'M WRONG?!

GRAB

HA HA.

GOOD LUCK.

TAKE CARE, ASAGI! BE SAFE!

LET'S GO.

I GUESS...

MAYBE WE SHOULD TRY CLOSER TO THE ROAD.

OK.

TELL YOU WHAT. I'LL GO SCOUT THE BUSHES WHILE YOU GUYS TRY THE ROAD.

SILENCE

HUH?

GLANCE

DOES THIS MEAN...

WE'VE BEEN AROUND SO MANY OTHER PEOPLE LATELY.

IT'S JUST THE TWO OF US?!

BLUSH

YEAH. IT LOOKS GOOD... I GUESS YOU'RE MORE INTERESTED IN FOOD.

HA HA HA.

slump

?

ungh

ungh

HUH?

ASAGI.

BDMP

TA DA! CHECK IT OUT! A TASTY-LOOKING RABBIT!

flail

kick

UGH.

I SEE LOTS OF RABBITS.

WIPE

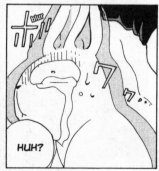

blur

HUH?

KAEDE!

hop

hop

hop

?!

THWUMP

SPIN-NING?!

EVERY-THING'S SPINNING...

UGH.

ARE YOU OK? YOU'VE BEEN ACTING WEIRD TODAY.

TAP

YOU'RE BURNING UP.

I...I DON'T WANNA BE A BURDEN.

WHOA. TAKE IT EASY.

I CAN WALK.

I'M OK.

STAGGER

WHAT'S WRONG?

?

OK.

I'M JUST WORRIED ABOUT YOU. DON'T LOOK SO SAD, OK? YOU'RE NOT A BURDEN.

SHE LOOKS PALE.

COME ON. LET'S REST SOMEWHERE. I HAVE SOME MEDICINE YOU CAN TAKE.

HERE. LET ME CARRY YOU.

UH...

WE SHOULD GO THIS WAY.

FORGET IT! THEY'RE THIS WAY!

GRRRR

THAT'S NOT WHAT I MEANT!

NOSE? WHAT ARE YOU NOW, A DOG?! ANYWAY, A **WOLF'S** NOSE IS A HUNDRED TIMES BETTER!

YOU'RE AN IDIOT!

SNAP!

ZAP!

I'M MORE SENSITIVE TO DEMONIC AURAS THAN YOU!

LOOK, I'VE GOT A NOSE FOR THIS KIND OF THING, ALRIGHT?

LET ME KNOW WHEN YOU'RE DONE, ALRIGHT?

YEAH, NICE LANGUAGE, TOOTS. REAL LADY-LIKE.

MUTT? YOU'RE ONE TO TALK, YOU HAIRY-ASS APE!

YOU'RE THE ONE WHO DOESN'T MAKE SENSE, YOU MANGY MUTT!

THEN WHAT **DID** YOU MEAN? YOU DON'T MAKE ANY SENSE!

JEEZ

chirp

chirp

UH-OH. WHERE THE HELL AM I?

OK.

TAKE THIS. IT'LL MAKE YOU FEEL BETTER.

OH.

NO.

I'M OUT OF WATER. DO YOU HAVE ANY?

WE PASSED A STREAM A LITTLE WAYS BACK, DIDN'T WE?

OK.

WAIT HERE. I'LL BE BACK IN A MINUTE.

サ・ワ...
RUSTLE

!

?!

MEANWHILE

I DON'T EVEN KNOW WHERE I CAME FROM.

びょん
leap

I AM SERIOUSLY LOST.

AAAUGH!

WHAT WAS THAT?!

SPLASH

KAEDE?!

THAT VOICE!

DASH

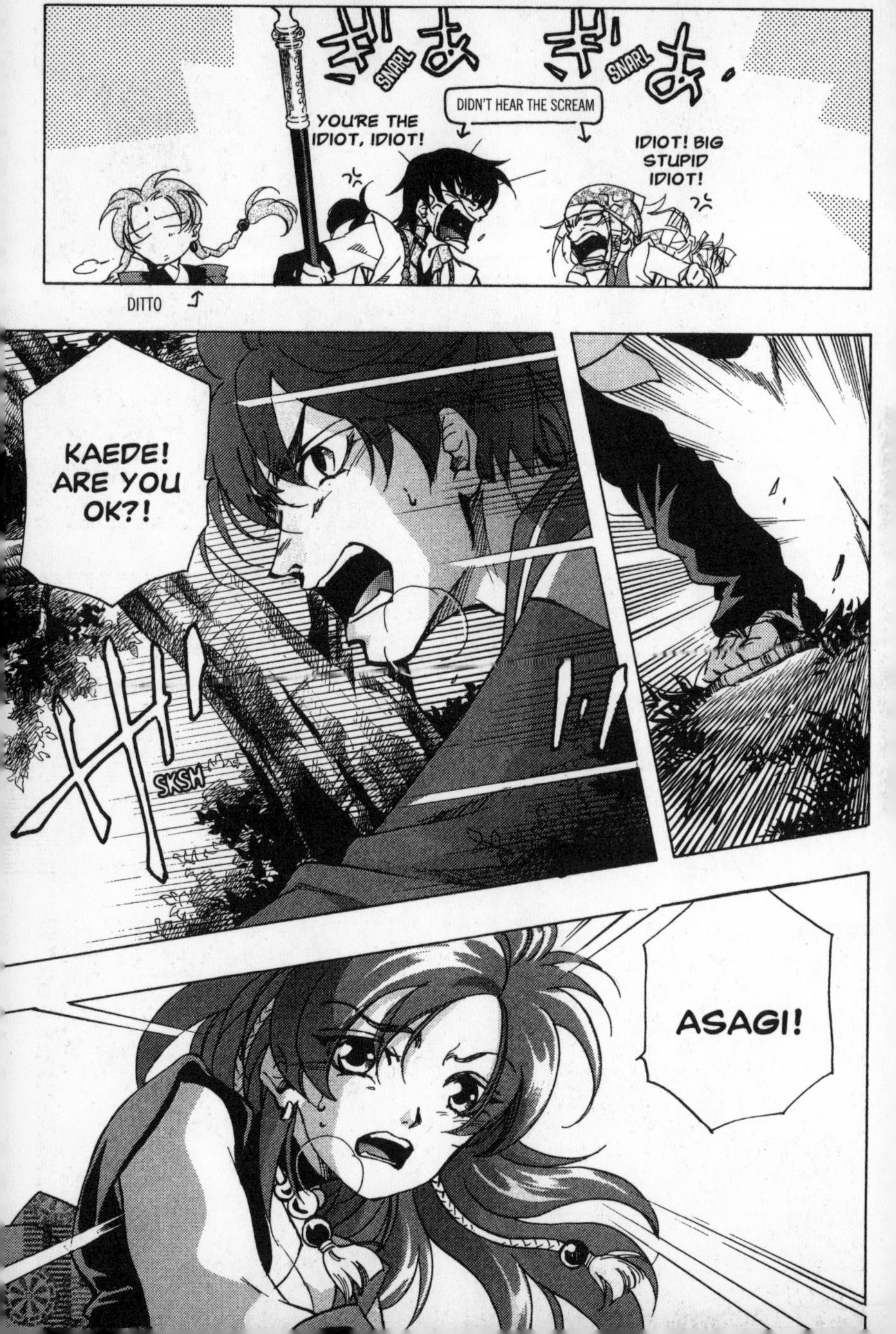
SNARL
SNARL
DIDN'T HEAR THE SCREAM
IDIOT! BIG STUPID IDIOT!
YOU'RE THE IDIOT, IDIOT!
DITTO
KAEDE! ARE YOU OK?!
SKSH
ASAGI!

RUSTLE

WHAT THE?!

IT LOOKS LIKE THAT TREE'S GOING TO ATTACK!

ATTACK?!

WHAT IS THIS?

IT'S MOVING.

VWOOSH

FWOOSH

SHPAK

GLARE

DAMMIT!

SHK

ZWSH

IT...IT'S BLEEDING!

IT'S A JUBOKKO!*

NOW I GET IT!

*A tree that has tasted human blood, turning it into a demon. It catches people and sucks their blood.

THESE THINGS LIVE OFF OF HUMAN BLOOD.

THIS COULD BE AN OLD BATTLE-GROUND.

IT'S NOT FAR FROM THE ROAD, EITHER. THIS IS PROBABLY WHAT ATTACKED ALL THOSE MISSING VILLAGERS.

WHOOSH

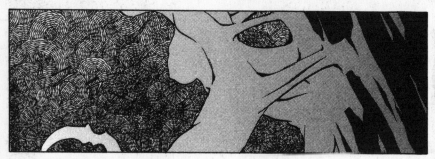

AAAUGH!

SLASH

SLASH

SLASH

SQUEEZE

KAEDE!

LET GO OF HER...

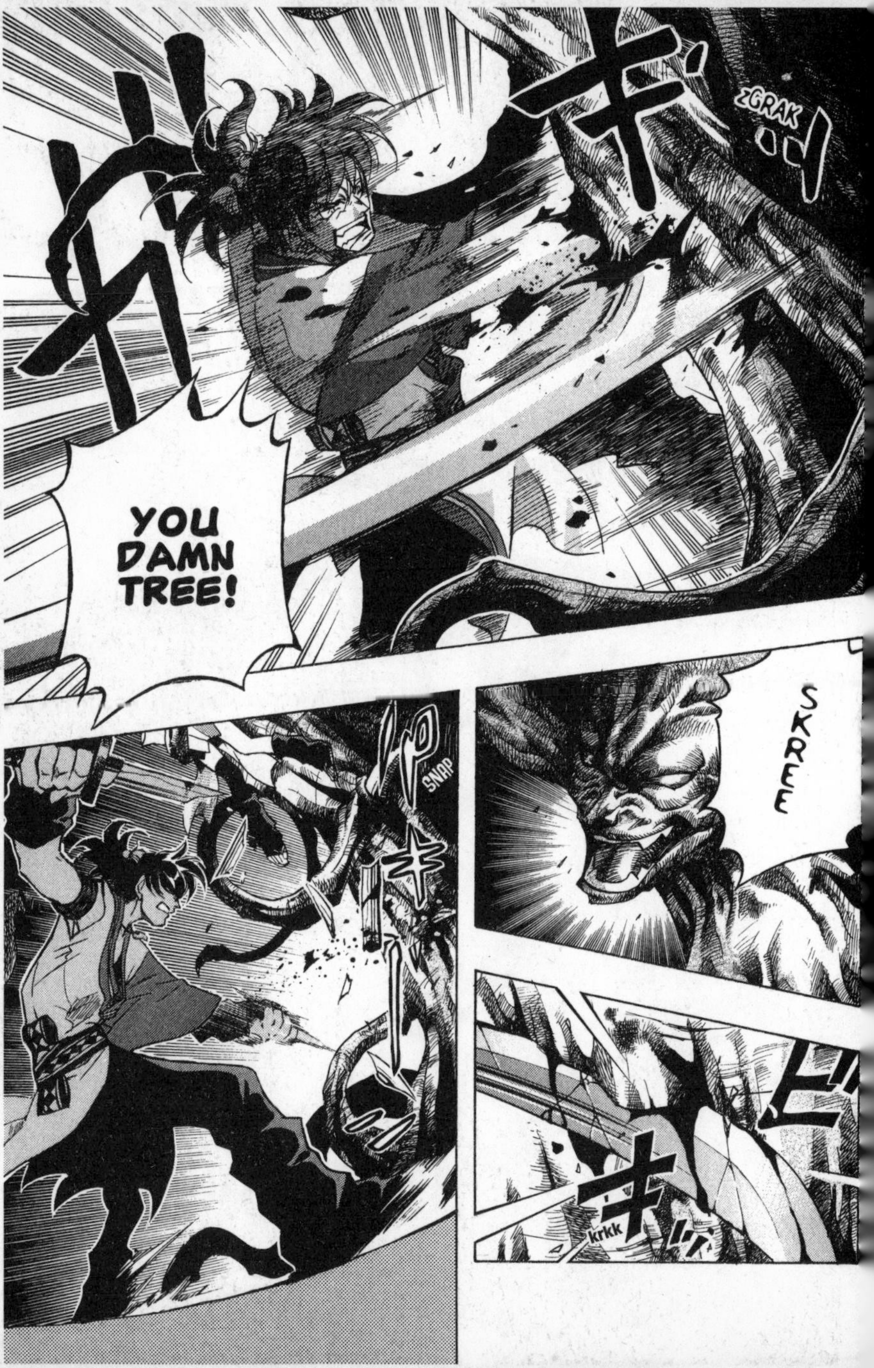

GRAK
YOU DAMN TREE!
SKREE
SNAP
krkk

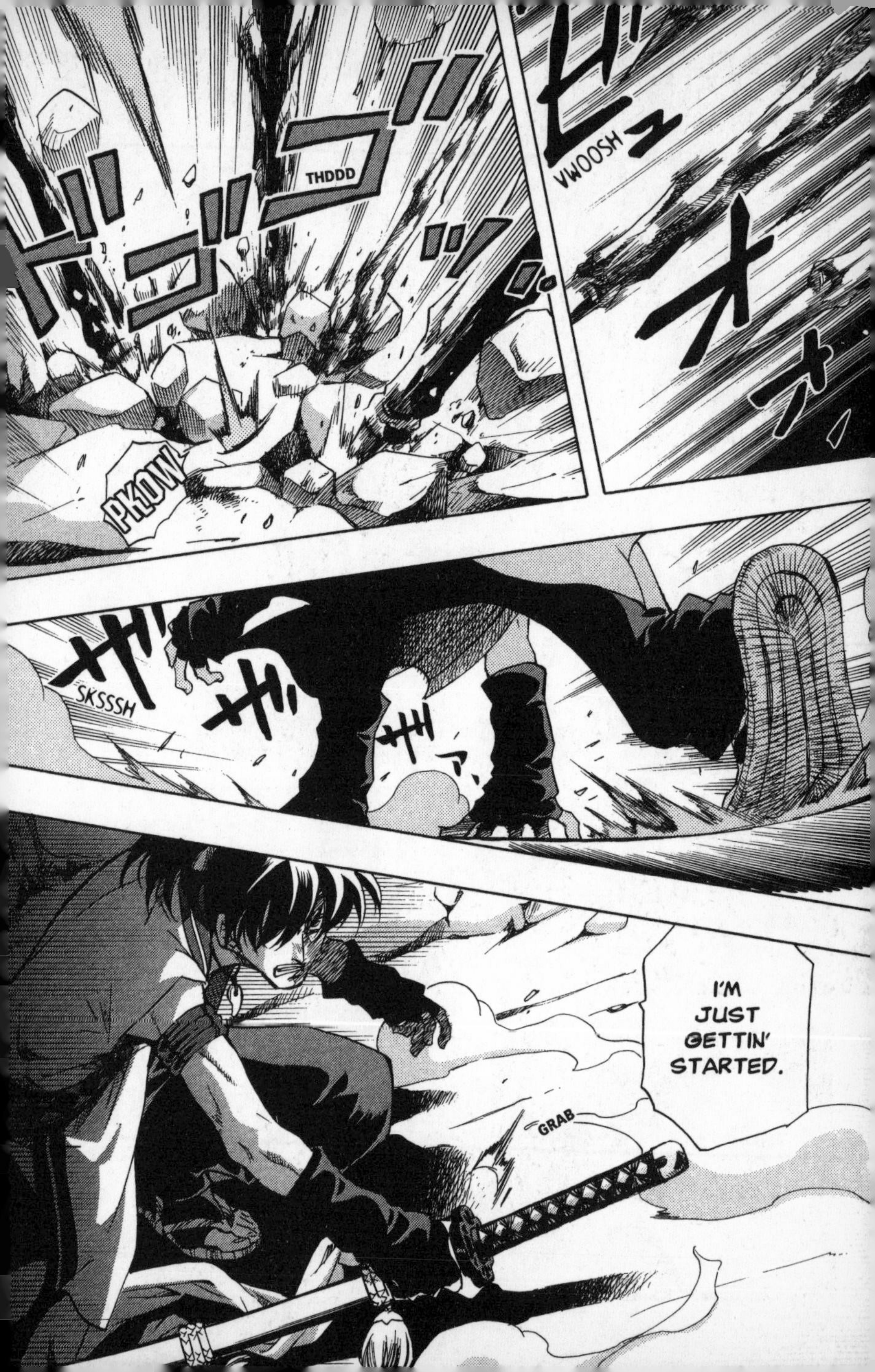
VWOOSH
THDDD
PKOW
SKSSSH
I'M JUST GETTIN' STARTED.
GRAB

KCHK

KAEDE!

AUGH!

SQUEEZE

ASAGI...

DAMN. IF I DRAW THE MOEGI, KAEDE MIGHT NOT BE ABLE TO HANDLE IT.

ARE YOU ALRIGHT?!

DO IT, ASAGI!

VWOOSH!

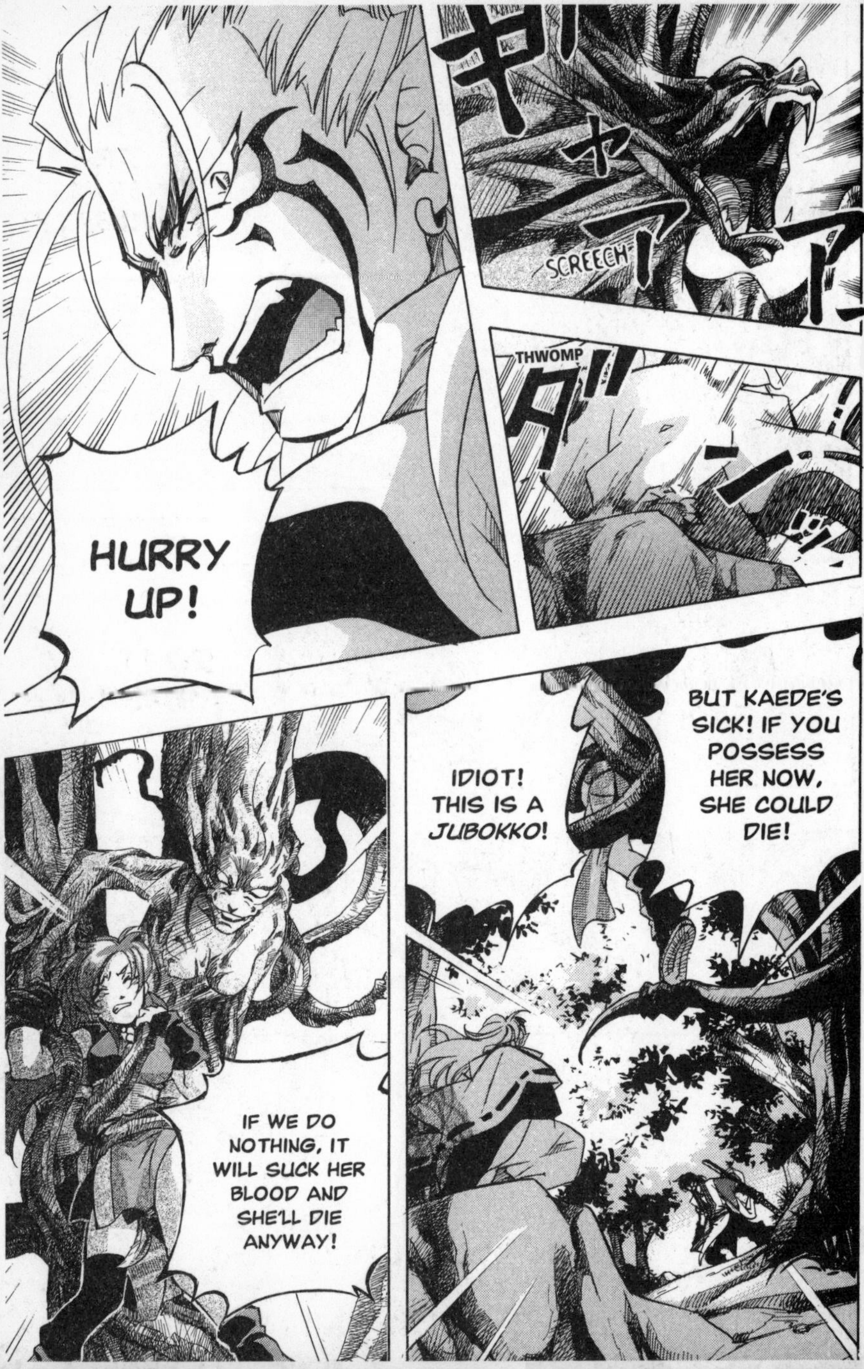
SCREECH
THWOMP
HURRY UP!
BUT KAEDE'S SICK! IF YOU POSSESS HER NOW, SHE COULD DIE!
IDIOT! THIS IS A JUBOKKO!
IF WE DO NOTHING, IT WILL SUCK HER BLOOD AND SHE'LL DIE ANYWAY!

BUT--

SHUT UP AND DO IT!

MY DAUGHTER'S NO WEAKLING, ASAGI!

FINE, BUT IF SHE DIES BECAUSE OF THIS...

THERE'S GONNA BE HELL TO PAY.

PSHK

VWOOSH

HEH. RIGHT BACK AT YOU.

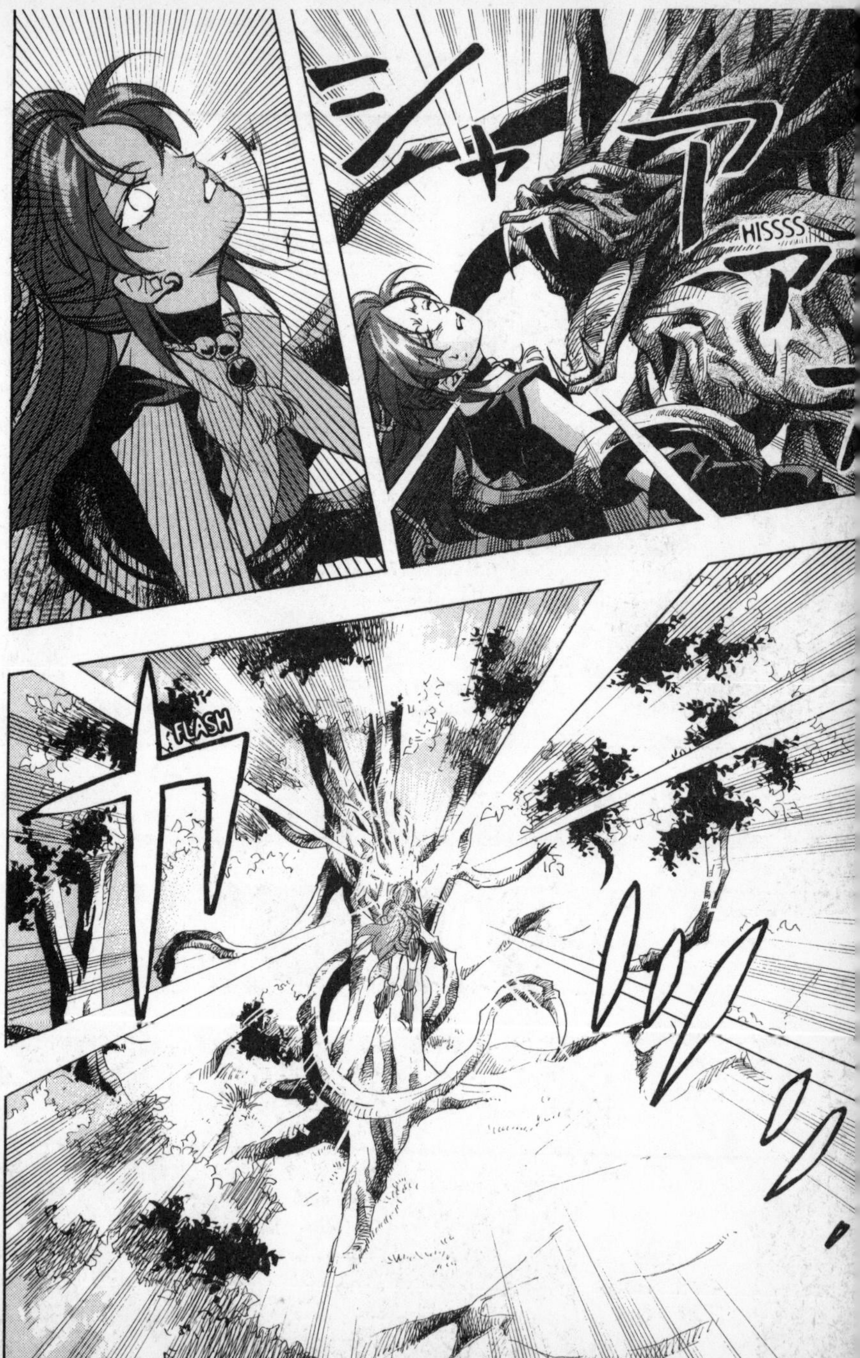

HISSSS
FLASH

grghh

BWAM

STUPID
BLOOD-
SUCKING
TREE.

I GOT
SOMETHING
FOR YOU!

AND I DON'T THINK YOU'RE GONNA LIKE IT.

GRIN

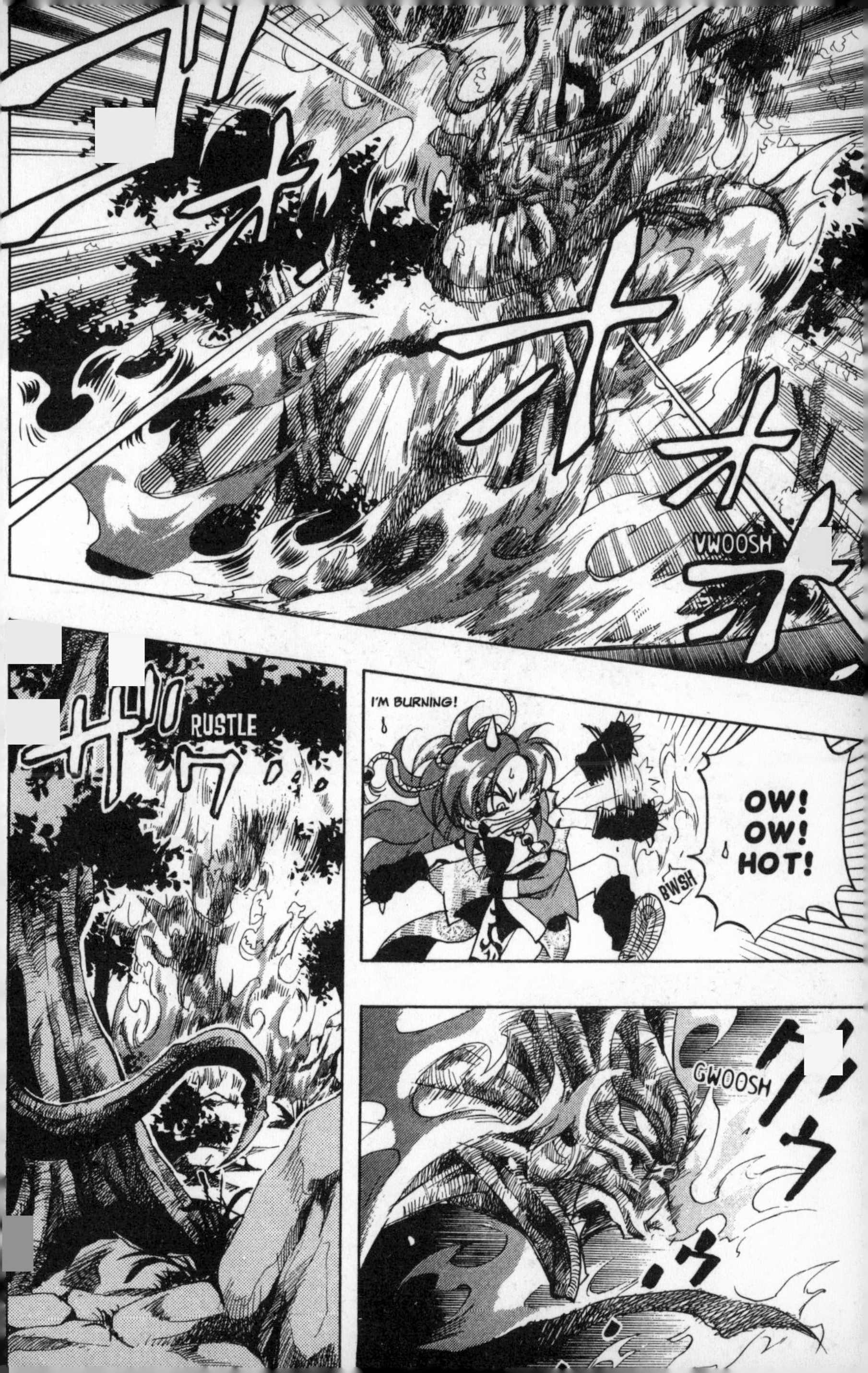
VWOOSH
I'M BURNING!
OW! OW! HOT!
BWSH
GWOOSH
RUSTLE

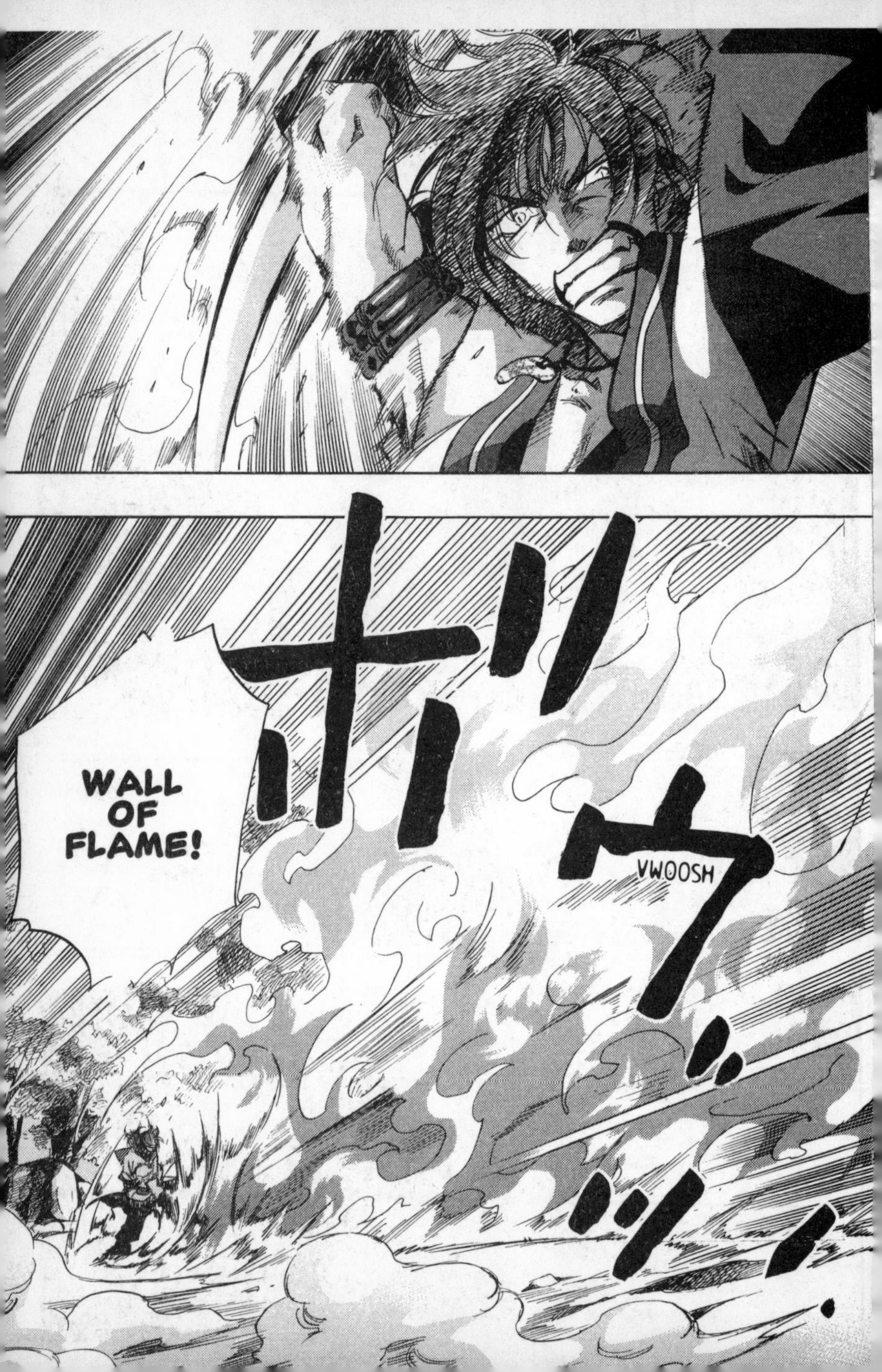
WALL OF FLAME!
VWOOSH

DAMN!

I'M ALL TAPPED OUT!

SWOOSH

GET BACK!

GRAB

SCUFF

TOTTER

≡PANT≡

≡GASP≡

≡PANT≡

KAEDE'S BODY FEELS HEAVY. SHE'S SO WORN OUT, I CAN'T EVEN DRAW ENOUGH POWER TO SHOOT FIRE.

SCREECH

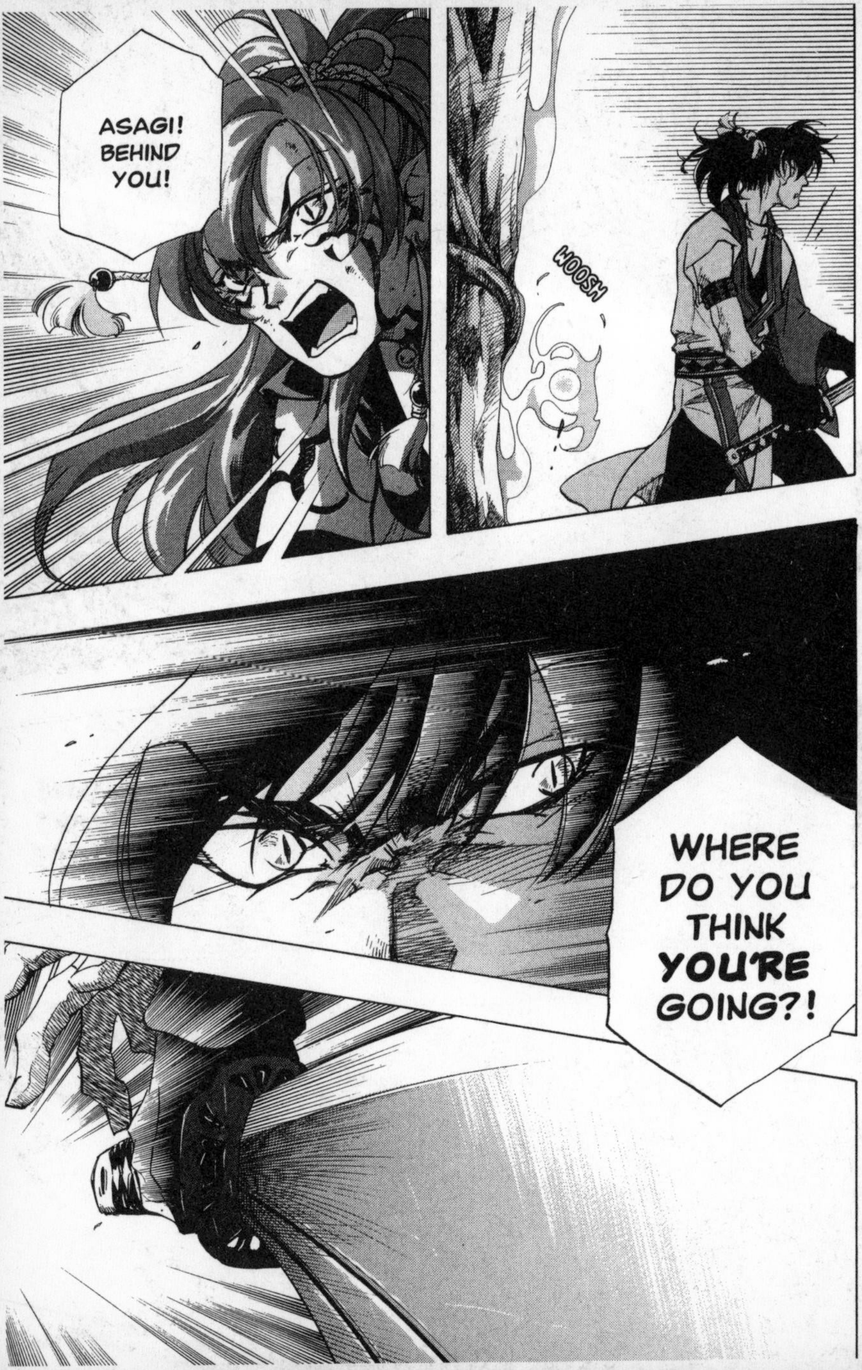
WOOSH
ASAGI! BEHIND YOU!
WHERE DO YOU THINK YOU'RE GOING?!

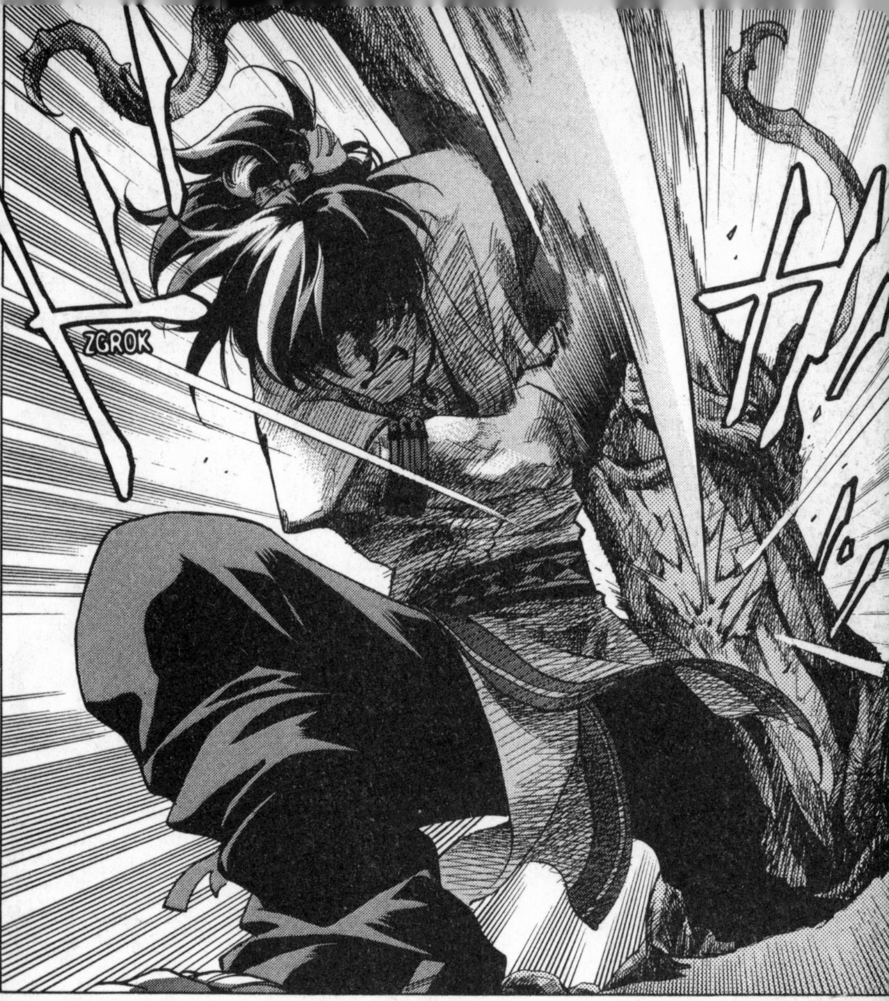
ZGROK
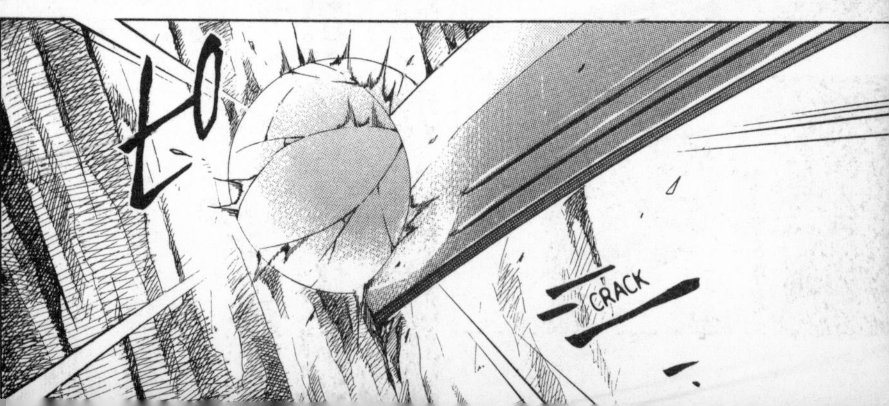
CRACK

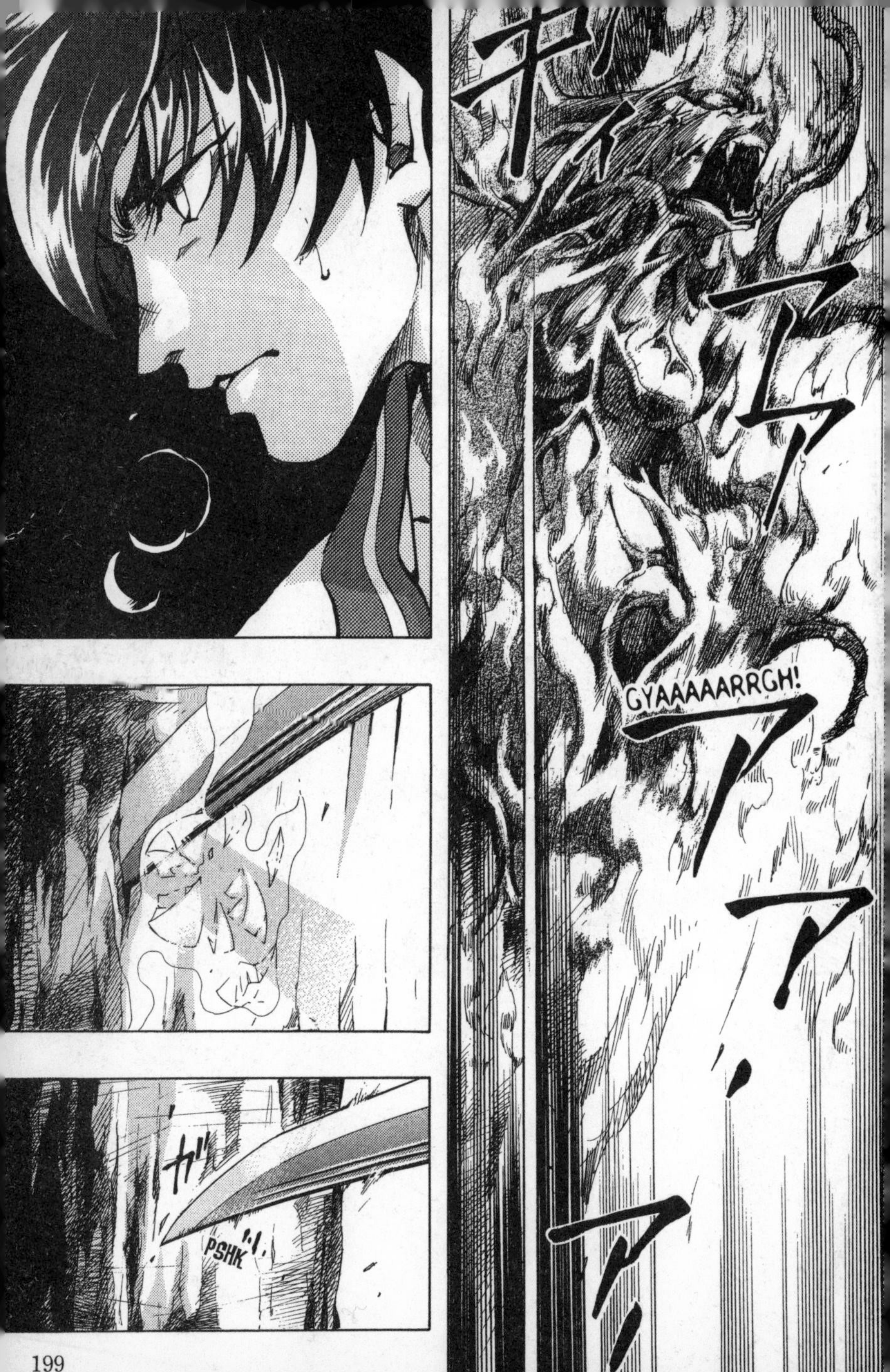
GYAAAAARRGH!
PSHK

chik

RANGER OFFICE—IWAMI BRANCH

WHAT ARE YOU WORRIED ABOUT? IT'S JUST A COLD.

THANK GOODNESS. HER FEVER'S GONE DOWN.

YUP, THIS ONE'S NO WEAKLING. I GUESS SHE TAKES AFTER HER DAD.

HEH.

OBVIOUSLY.

GRIN

YEAH...

ANYWAY, WHERE'S EVERYBODY ELSE?

IT'S ALREADY DARK.

DO YOU FEEL THAT? THERE'S SOMETHING COMING.

AT LEAST THE BOUNTY FROM THAT *JUBOKKO* IS ENOUGH TO PAY FOR A DECENT MEAL.

WE **DID** MAKE OUT PRETTY GOOD.

OR SOME- THING.

LIKE A BALL OF DEMONIC ENERGY IS FLYING TOWARD US.

A BALL?!

NO, WHAT IS IT?

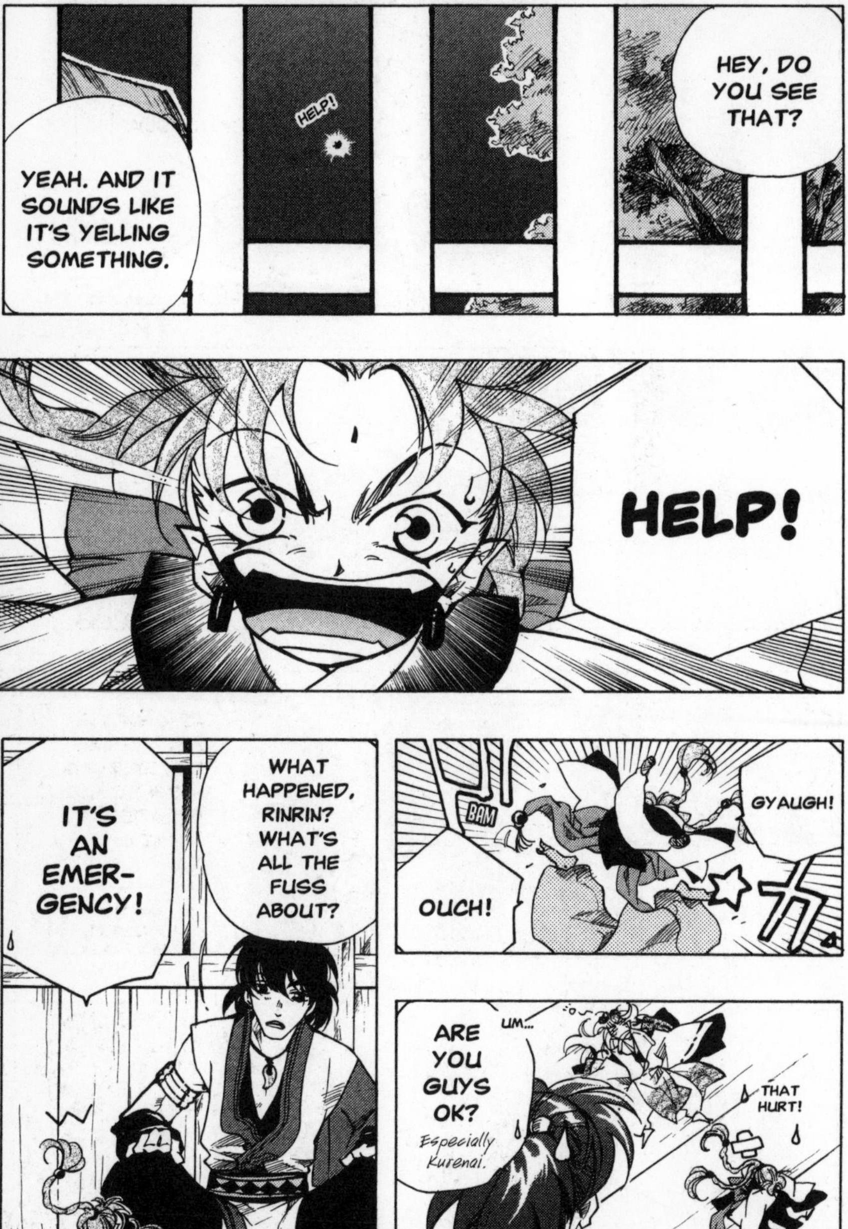
HEY, DO YOU SEE THAT?
HELP!
YEAH. AND IT SOUNDS LIKE IT'S YELLING SOMETHING.
HELP!
BAM
GYAUGH!
OUCH!
ARE YOU GUYS OK?
Especially Kurenai.
UM...
THAT HURT!
WHAT HAPPENED, RINRIN? WHAT'S ALL THE FUSS ABOUT?
IT'S AN EMER-GENCY!

SUOH AND AOI ARE IN TROUBLE!

HUH?!

CHAPTER 4: JUBOKKO / THE END

POSTSCRIPT

Thank you for buying *By the Sword*. It's taken a while to release volume 2, but I'm happy to say that we finally did it.

The reason for the delay was that we were just short of our page count, and needed one more installment's worth before we could finally publish it. Many of you were kind enough to write in and ask about the status of this volume--and at last, the wait is over!

When this first ran in *Magazine Zero*, there were color pages as well as a color fold-out, which was a refreshing change.

For the graphic novel, we hired a professional designer to do the Table of Contents page, which I'm very pleased with. (I was given two different patterns to choose from, and went with the one you see here because the carp was so pretty.)

The covers for volumes 1 and 2 feature all new illustrations. Let me know what you think!

I also have a homepage, so take a look.
www.sanami-matoh.com

Matoh

SW**O**RD BY THE 2

(Originally published as "YO-U" in Japan.)

© 2003 by SANAMI MATOH/BIBLOS
Originally published in Japan in 2003 by BIBLOS Co., Ltd.

Translator **YUKO YOSHIKAWA**
Translation Staff **KAY BERTRAND, AMY FORSYTH AND BRENDAN FRAYNE**
Editor **JAVIER LOPEZ**
Assistant Editor **SHERIDAN JACOBS**
Graphic Artists **HEATHER GARY AND NATALIA REYNOLDS**
Graphic Intern **MARK MEZA**

Editorial Director **GARY STEINMAN**
Creative Director **JASON BABLER**
Sales and Marketing **CHRIS OARR**
Print Production Manager **BRIDGETT JANOTA**
Pre-press Manager **KLYS REEDYK**

International Coordinators **TORU IWAKAMI, ATSUSHI KANBAYASHI,
KYOKO DRUMHELLER AND AI TAKAI**

President, CEO & Publisher **JOHN LEDFORD**

Email: editor@adv-manga.com
www.adv-manga.com
www.advfilms.com

For sales and distribution inquiries please call 1.800.282.7202

ADV MANGA is a division of A.D. Vision, Inc.
10114 W. Sam Houston Parkway, Suite 200, Houston, Texas 77099

English text © 2005 published by A.D. Vision, Inc. under exclusive license.
ADV MANGA is a trademark of A.D. Vision, Inc.

ISBN: 1-4139-0214-6
First printing, June 2005
10 9 8 7 6 5 4 3 2 1
Printed in Canada

By The Sword Vol. 02

 Dragon kings and mermaids

While these two would appear to have little in common, they aren't actually as disparate as it initially seems. In Japanese folklore, it's not at all uncommon for dragons to live in the ocean. The story of Urashima Taro, for example, features a dragon king whose palace is located beneath the waves.

 The dragon orb

In mythology, dragons are often said to be in possession of a pearl or an orb. An example of this is the Chinese folk tale of Xiao Sheng, in which a boy finds a pearl that holds magical properties. When he swallows the pearl and later drinks from a river to quench the terrible thirst that ensues, he transforms into a dragon that brings much-needed rain to his village.

 Sen

This monetary unit, now obsolete, was worth about 1/100 of a yen. Mention of it remains in the somewhat colorful phrase *issen mo nai*, which means to not have a penny to one's name (lit. "not even a single *sen*").

Sinister looks and foxes

Fox spirits, or *kitsune* in Japanese, possess a variety of magical powers, including the ability to metamorphose at will. They are also regarded as shrewd and beguilers of unsuspecting humans, hence the comment about having a "sinister look." The word *kitsune* is a blanket term encompassing all forms of fox spirits—there are said to be thirteen separate varieties.

Kuko

Kuko are fox spirits generally associated with air or mist. While they are said to be the most wicked of all *kitsune*, Rindo would seem to be the exception to this rule.

EDITOR'S

PICKS

PICK 1

© Nanae Chrono 2002

PEACEMAKER KUROGANE

Tetsunosuke Ichimura has finally joined the ranks of the Shinsengumi, feudal Kyoto's samurai police. As a page for Vice-Commander Hijikata, he has been made privy to both Japan's highest ranking officials and their secrets! With this responsibility comes the all important duty of protection, and when a certain enemy threatens the city, the Shinsengumi—and Tetsunosuke—draw their swords, swiftly serving up justice as the dueling protectors of the embattled imperial capital.

PICK 2

© WATARU MURAYAMA 2002

DESERT CORAL

Naoto Saki has an imagination so far-reaching that he has found an entire world within his dreams, filled with fascinating creatures and longstanding rivalries. After days and nights of escaping reality, he is summoned to this illusory land and into a battle between the Elphis and the Sand Dusts. Pain is real here, but the risk of certain injury and even death will not stave his eventual attachment to this world of fantasy. Naoto will ultimately be faced with a decision that will forever change him and the fate of *Desert Coral*.

PICK 3

© MAKI HAKODA 2003

R²

Life for Kenta Akagi is safe, stable and altogether uneventful. Born and raised in the remote city of Lutzheim, he can only wonder what strange and wonderful creatures exist, or how battles are fought and won. A life of excitement is unknown to young Kenta, until he is whisked away to a foreign land. He becomes a warrior, fighting for possession of a girl, but he doesn't know who or what this girl is. He only senses that he must protect her, even if it causes more destruction than peace...

CHECK 'EM OUT TODAY!

ADV MANGA™

www.adv-manga.com

FROM THE CREATOR OF *AZUMANGA DAIOH!*

YOTSUBA&!

①

THE LAUGHTER BEGINS **JUNE 2005**

KIYOHIKO AZUMA

A NEW SERIES FROM **KIYOHIKO AZUMA!**

INTERNATIONAL BEST-SELLING AUTHOR OF **AZUMANGA DAIOH**

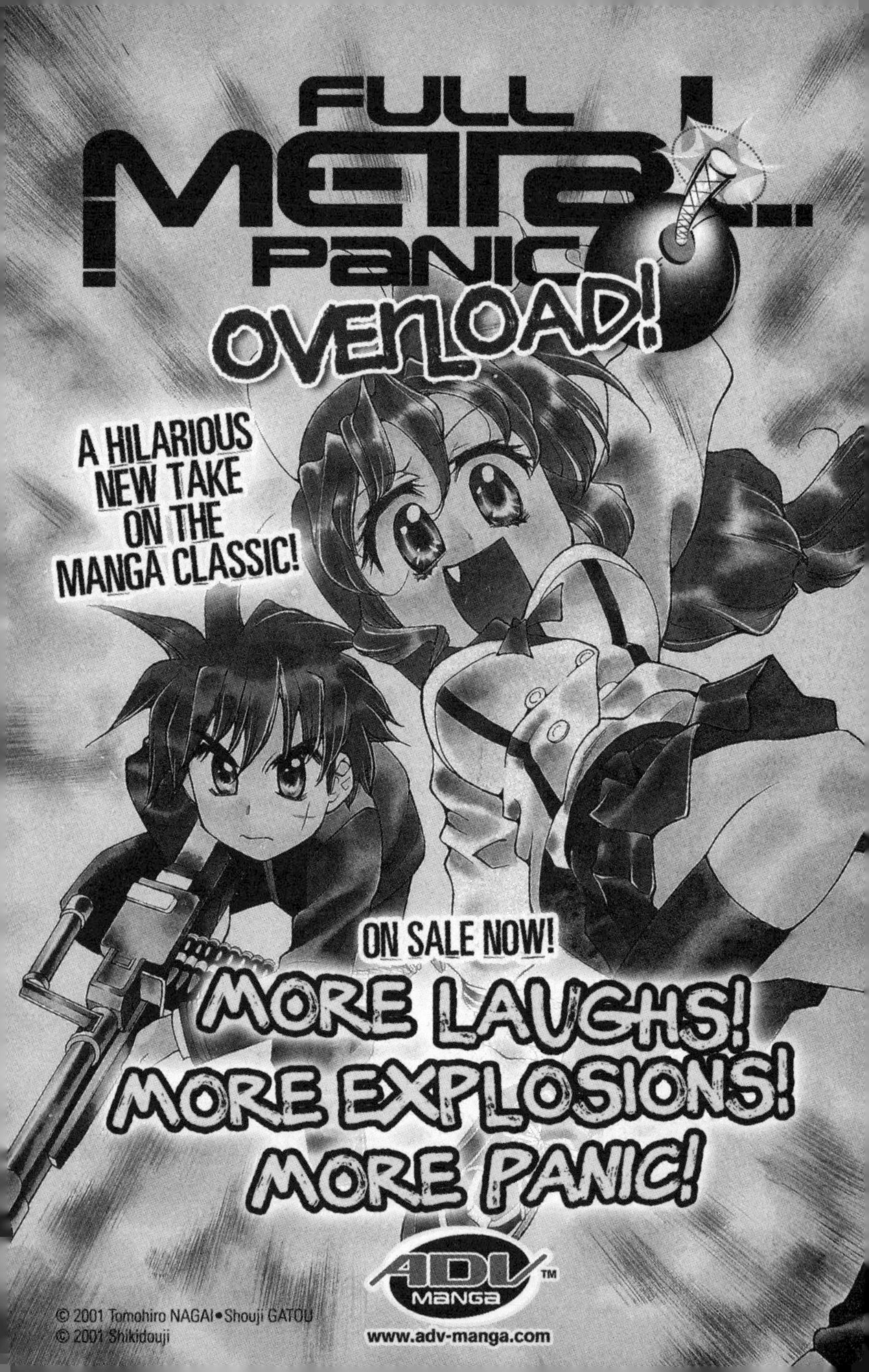

FULL METAL PANIC
OVERLOAD!
A HILARIOUS NEW TAKE ON THE MANGA CLASSIC!
ON SALE NOW!
MORE LAUGHS!
MORE EXPLOSIONS!
MORE PANIC!
ADV Manga ™
© 2001 Tomohiro NAGAI • Shouji GATOU
© 2001 Shikidouji
www.adv-manga.com

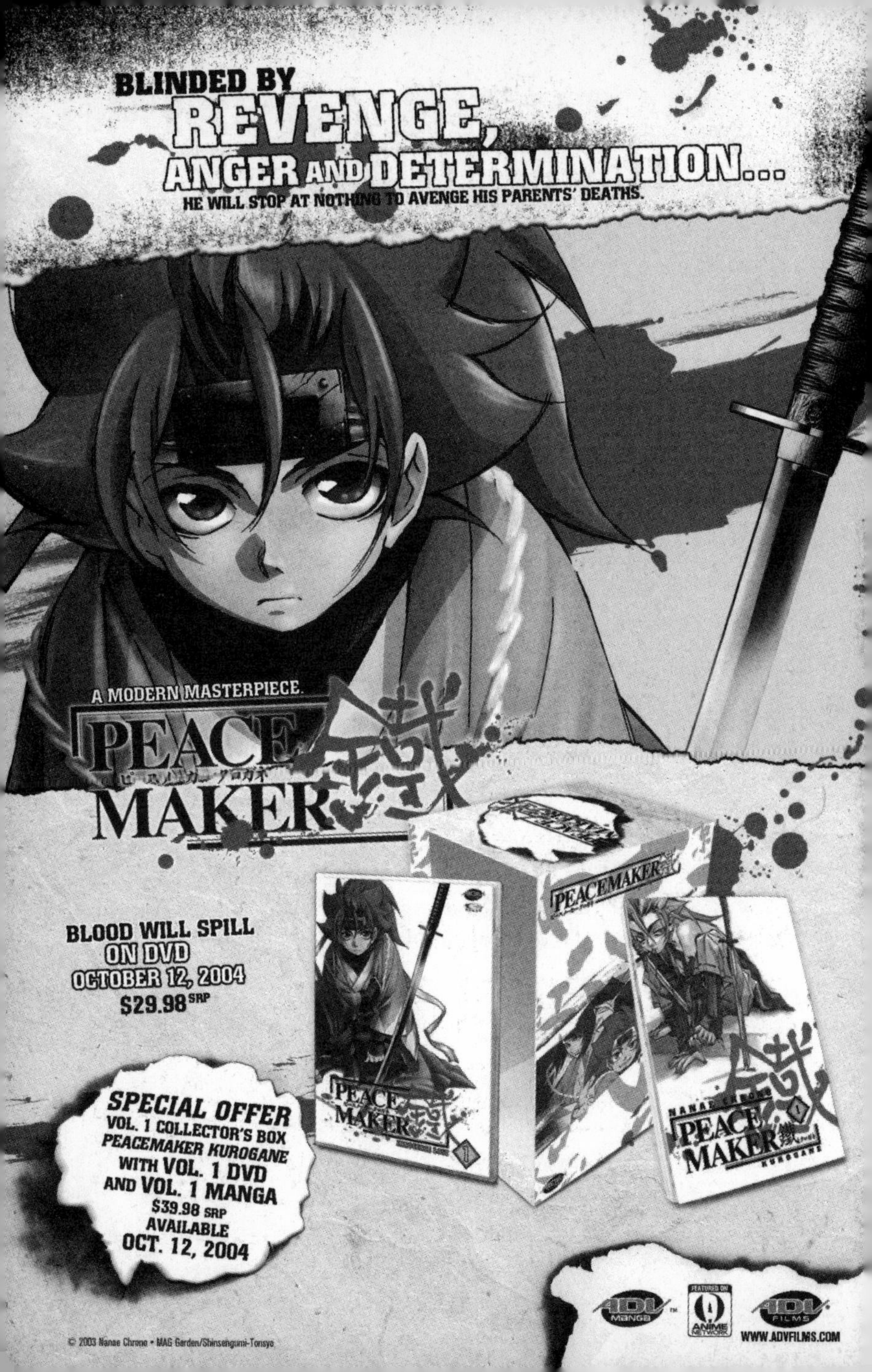

BLINDED BY
REVENGE,
ANGER AND DETERMINATION...
HE WILL STOP AT NOTHING TO AVENGE HIS PARENTS' DEATHS.
A MODERN MASTERPIECE.
PEACE MAKER
BLOOD WILL SPILL
ON DVD
OCTOBER 12, 2004
$29.98 SRP
SPECIAL OFFER
VOL. 1 COLLECTOR'S BOX
PEACEMAKER KUROGANE
WITH VOL. 1 DVD
AND VOL. 1 MANGA
$39.98 SRP
AVAILABLE
OCT. 12, 2004
PEACEMAKER
PEACE MAKER
PEACE MAKER
KUROGANE
© 2003 Nanae Chrono • MAG Garden/Shinsengumi-Tonsyo
WWW.ADVFILMS.COM

COMETHING MICCING
FROM YOUR TV?

ROBOT DESTRUCTION

SAMURAI VIOLENCE

KAWAII OVERDOSE

SKIMPY CLOTHES

NOSE BLEEDING

SUPER DEFORMED CHARACTERS

UPSKIRTS

EXTREME JIGGLING

HYPERACTIVE TEENS

MONSTER RAMPAGE

METROPOLITAN MELTDOWN

BLOOD & GUTS

Tired of networks that only dabble in anime? Tired of the same old cartoons?

Demand more from your cable or satellite operator. If they don't currently offer Anime Network as part of your channel lineup, then something is missing.

Your TV deserves better.

You deserve Anime Network.

Log on and demand anime in your home 24/7:
WWW.THEANIMENETWORK.COM

ANIME
NETWORK.

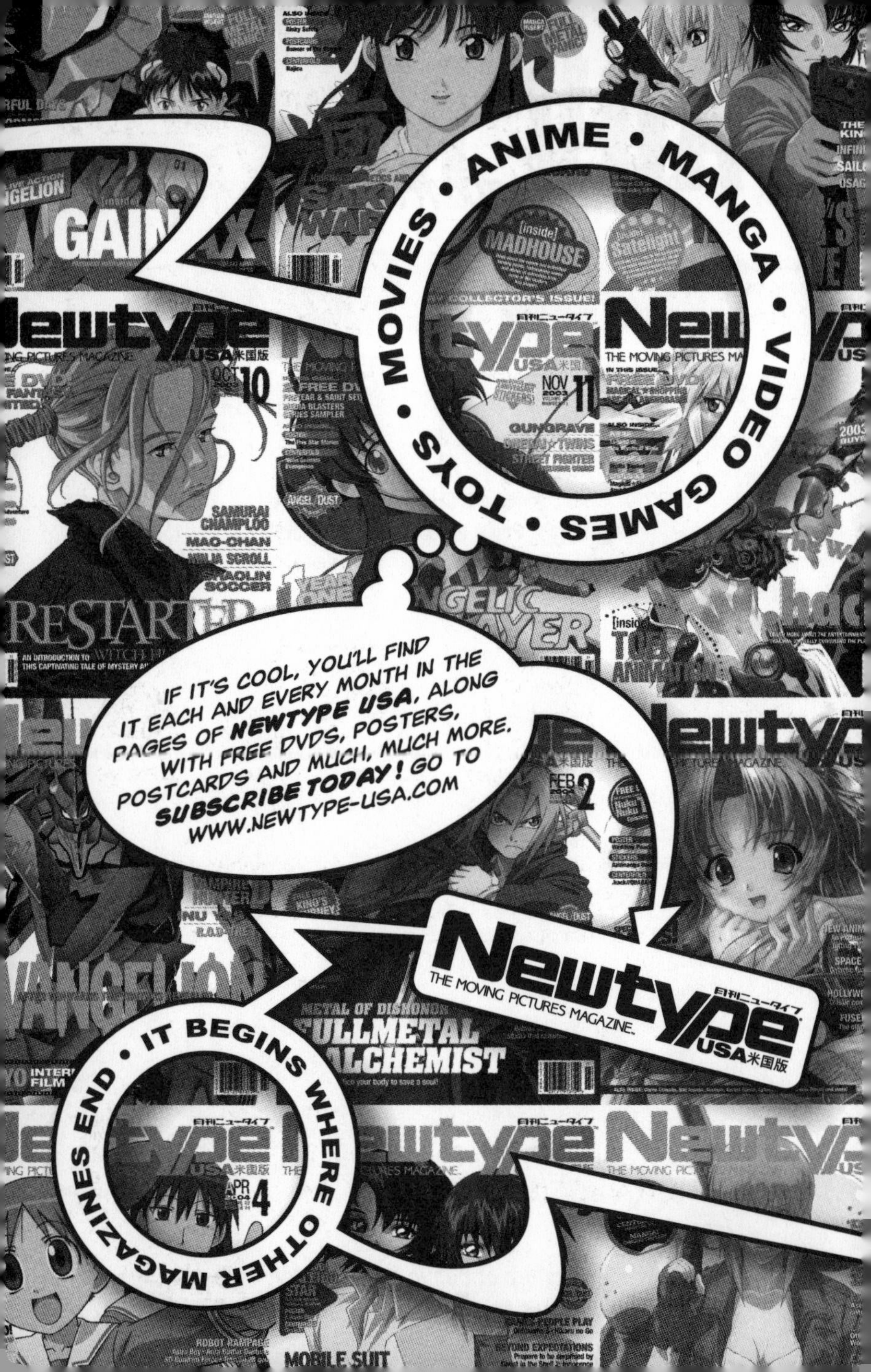
MOVIES • ANIME • MANGA • VIDEO GAMES • TOYS •
IF IT'S COOL, YOU'LL FIND IT EACH AND EVERY MONTH IN THE PAGES OF NEWTYPE USA, ALONG WITH FREE DVDS, POSTERS, POSTCARDS AND MUCH, MUCH MORE. SUBSCRIBE TODAY! GO TO WWW.NEWTYPE-USA.COM
Newtype USA
THE MOVING PICTURES MAGAZINE.
IT BEGINS WHERE OTHER MAGAZINES END •

MANGA *you'll want them all!*

50 Rules for Teenagers
All Purpose Cultural Cat Girl
 Nuku Nuku
Apocalypse Meow
Aria
Azumanga Daioh
Blue Inferior
By the Sword
Chrono Crusade
Cromartie High School
Daemon Hunters
Dark Water
Darkside Blues
Demon City Hunter
Demon City Shinjuku
Demon Palace Babylon
Desert Coral
Dream Gold
Enmusu
Fantasy Land
Figure 17
The First King Adventure
Full Metal Panic!
Full Metal Panic! Film Book
Gadirok
Gadget
Gamerz Heaven
Gate
Gunparade March
Gunslinger Girl

Happy Lesson
Jinki: Extend
Kagerou-Nostalgia:
 The Resurrection
Kids Joker
Louie the Rune Soldier
Maburaho
More Starlight to Your Heart
Mystical Prince Yoshida-kun!
Mythical Detective
 LOKI Ragnarok
Najica Blitz Tactics
Noodle Fighter Miki
Orphen
Peacemaker Kurogane
Prétear
Princess Tutu
Quantum Mistake
RahXephon Bible
 Illustration Book
R^2
Ray
The Ruler of the Land
Saint Marie
Seven of Seven
Sky Blade:
 Sword of the Heavens
Steel Angel Kurumi
Sweet & Sensitive
Tactics

Taimashin
Tengai-Retrogical
The Boss
The First King Adventure
Those Who Hunt Elves
To Heart
Vaizard
YOTSUBA&!
Your and My Secret

Available at your local bookstore or comic book retailer,
or visit us online at www.adv-manga.com.

www.adv-manga.com

MANGA SURVEY

PLEASE MAIL THE COMPLETED FORM TO: EDITOR – ADV MANGA
℅ A.D. Vision, Inc. 10114 W. Sam Houston Pkwy., Suite 200 Houston, TX 77099

Name:_____

Address:_____

City, State, Zip:_____

_____

E-Mail:_____

Male ☐   Female ☐   Age:_____

☐ **CHECK HERE IF YOU WOULD LIKE TO RECEIVE OTHER INFORMATION OR FUTURE OFFERS FROM ADV.**

All information provided will be used for internal purposes only. We promise not to sell or otherwise divulge your information.

1. Annual Household Income (*Check only one*)
- ☐ Under $25,000
- ☐ $25,000 to $50,000
- ☐ $50,000 to $75,000
- ☐ Over $75,000

2. How do you hear about new Manga releases? (*Check all that apply*)
- ☐ Browsing in Store
- ☐ Internet Reviews
- ☐ Anime News Websites
- ☐ Direct Email Campaigns
- ☐ Magazine Ad
- ☐ Online Advertising
- ☐ Conventions
- ☐ TV Advertising
- ☐ Online forums (message boards and chat rooms)
- ☐ Carrier pigeon
- ☐ Other:_____

3. Which magazines do you read? (*Check all that apply*)
- ☐ Wizard
- ☐ SPIN
- ☐ Animerica
- ☐ Rolling Stone
- ☐ Maxim
- ☐ DC Comics
- ☐ URB
- ☐ Polygon
- ☐ Official PlayStation Magazine
- ☐ Entertainment Weekly
- ☐ YRB
- ☐ EGM
- ☐ Newtype USA
- ☐ SciFi
- ☐ Starlog
- ☐ Wired
- ☐ Vice
- ☐ BPM
- ☐ I hate reading
- ☐ Other:_____

4. **Have you visited the ADV Manga website?**
- ☐ Yes
- ☐ No

5. **Have you made any manga purchases online from the ADV website?**
- ☐ Yes
- ☐ No

6. **If you have visited the ADV Manga website, how would you rate your online experience?**
- ☐ Excellent
- ☐ Good
- ☐ Average
- ☐ Poor

7. **What genre of manga do you prefer?**
(*Check all that apply*)
- ☐ adventure
- ☐ romance
- ☐ detective
- ☐ action
- ☐ horror
- ☐ sci-fi/fantasy
- ☐ sports
- ☐ comedy

8. **How many manga titles have you purchased in the last 6 months?**
- ☐ none
- ☐ 1-4
- ☐ 5-10
- ☐ 11+

9. **Where do you make your manga purchases?** (*Check all that apply*)
- ☐ comic store
- ☐ bookstore
- ☐ newsstand
- ☐ online
- ☐ other:_____
- ☐ department store
- ☐ grocery store
- ☐ video store
- ☐ video game store

10. **Which bookstores do you usually make your manga purchases at?**
(*Check all that apply*)
- ☐ Barnes & Noble
- ☐ Walden Books
- ☐ Suncoast
- ☐ Best Buy
- ☐ Amazon.com
- ☐ Borders
- ☐ Books-A-Million
- ☐ Toys "Я" Us
- ☐ Other bookstore: _____

11. **What's your favorite anime/manga website?** (*Check all that apply*)
- ☐ adv-manga.com
- ☐ advfilms.com
- ☐ rightstuf.com
- ☐ animenewsservice.com
- ☐ animenewsnetwork.com
- ☐ Other:_____
- ☐ animeondvd.com
- ☐ anipike.com
- ☐ animeonline.net
- ☐ planetanime.com
- ☐ animenation.com